riting

L
26/11/07

What is creative writing? How, and why, do you do it?

Cr
to
at
Dc
cre

•

•

•

CANCELLED
MAY 2008

Dc
wh
alc
co
gre
ref
rea

St
Ui
cre
20

Doing Creative Writing

Steve May

Routledge
Taylor & Francis Group

LONDON AND NEW YORK

First published 2007
by Routledge
2 Park Square, Milton Park, Abingdon, Oxon OX14 4RN

Simultaneously published in the USA and Canada
by Routledge
270 Madison Avenue, New York, NY 10016

Routledge is an imprint of the Taylor & Francis Group, an informa business

© 2007 Steve May

Typeset in Times New Roman by RefineCatch Limited, Bungay, Suffolk
Printed and bound in Great Britain by
TJ International Ltd, Padstow, Cornwall

British Library Cataloguing in Publication Data
A catalogue record for this book is available from the British Library

Library of Congress Cataloging in Publication Data
May, Steve, 1953–
Doing creative writing / Steve May.
p. cm.
Includes bibliographical references and index.
1. English language—Rhetoric—Problems, exercises etc.
2. Creative writing—Problems, exercises, etc.   I. Title.
PE1408.M387   2007
808′.042071—dc22
2007028447

ISBN10: 0–415–40238–7 (hbk)
ISBN10: 0–415–40239–5 (pbk)
ISBN10: 0–203–93982–4 (ebk)

ISBN13: 978–0–415–40238–5 (hbk)
ISBN13: 978–0–415–40239–2 (pbk)
ISBN13: 978–0–203–93982–6 (ebk)

For Miriam, no better editor

Contents

Part III
Writers' habits, writers' skills

Foreword

Doing Creative Writing has been a long time coming. Creative Writing programmes have been growing at a rapid pace since the 1950s and 1960s in both the US and the UK, with arguably the greatest surge occurring post 1990 – and yet students have had to navigate this complex, somewhat mystery-shrouded path of study virtually without a compass. Until now.

Certainly, any number of useful handbooks about creative writing itself have appeared in the last 20 years, books that have gone a long way towards leading students around the writing mis-steps common to beginners. But until *Doing Creative Writing*, students electing to study this subject at university lacked a comprehensive guide to show them how to get the best out of their educations, and their courses.

In fact the forces that have inspired Steve May to write this student-centred guidebook speak volumes about the state of creative writing in universities today. As a field, creative writing in higher education has at last seen fit, in the past decade or so, to pause and reflect on just what it means to teach and learn creative writing. There has been a burst of scholarly energy focused on how to best equip creative writing students with the knowledge and skills that will sustain them in their post-university literary lives.

If you are a writer-educator, as I am, you hold in your hands a resource that stands to make your teaching life a good deal easier and your students even more savvy. I encourage you to urge them to make use of this volume by making it part of a course or programme of courses. I certainly plan to. If you are a student, I envy you. For as *Doing Creative Writing* epitomises, there is no better time in the history of creative writing to be setting out on your journey. Bon voyage!

Stephanie Vanderslice
Department of Writing
University of Central Arkansas

Acknowledgements

This book could not have been written without the input of students, particularly the Bath Spa CS1006 (Writing: The Process) cohort of October 2004: Suzanna Ball, Neil Ballantyne, Robyn Bowler, Dan Charles, Audrey Donaghue, Kristine Dukes, Gordon Eggington, Chris Elphick, Rebecca Fewings, Richard Fisher, Katie Gandy, Abigail Keverne, Emma Kirley, Emerson Leese, Edward Parshotam, Keely Rankin, Sam Reader, Claire Skuse, Helen Stone, Nicola Venables, Jamie Whear and Emma Wilson. My sincere thanks for their intelligence, enthusiasm, generosity and imagination.

Particular thanks are due to Dr Stephanie Vanderslice, Associate Professor of Creative Writing at the University of Central Arkansas, who read the manuscript and has generously put me right on several matters concerning the US creative writing context.

I'm also grateful to my colleagues at Bath Spa University for their sustained and passionate interest in the pedagogy of creative writing. Richard Kerridge, in particular, read early versions of the proposal for this book and gave valuable advice and criticism.

I have the English Subject Centre to thank for funding a research project into the teaching of creative writing at undergraduate level, which first raised the questions that I have tried to address in this book; my School for giving me relief from teaching in order to write it; and Helen for her forbearance and understanding when this writer's habits, skills and methods were proving less than effective.

General introduction

- Who is this book for?
- How will you benefit from it?
- What's in this book

Who is this book for?

If you're taking or thinking of taking any course in creative writing, this book will help you by introducing the key issues involved in the learning and teaching of that subject. In particular, if you're starting, thinking of starting or already taking a university course in creative writing, or a course that includes a creative writing element, *Doing Creative Writing* is for you.

By 'creative writing' I mean fiction, poetry, script, narrative non-fiction and the feature side of journalism (not news). By 'doing' I mean primarily taking an undergraduate course at a university or equivalent, but this book will also be of use to anyone considering a course in creative writing, as it covers such basic but crucial questions as: What does it mean to 'do' creative writing in practical terms? Can creative writing really be taught? How does 'creative' writing differ from other writing? What does a student of creative writing have to do, other than produce poems or stories or plays, and why? What might be the benefits of a formal creative writing course?

Because the focus in writing courses is very often on the *product* (the poems and stories etc.), and not on the complex *process* by which they are made, some people still look on creative writing as a 'soft option', perhaps thinking that all they have to do is sit in a comfortable chair and wait for inspiration to strike. The reality is rather different, and this book is designed to give you insight into that reality.

This book, on the one hand, invites you to explore why you want to 'do creative writing', and on the other outlines what you can expect to be *asked to do* as part of a course, and what you can expect to learn from it.

How will you benefit from it?

Recently I asked 75 students who had just completed the first semester of a university creative writing course what kind of book would have helped them get started and get more out of their course. One of the students wrote:

> *Not having any idea what to expect is quite nerve-wracking and background knowledge would have made workshops less intimidating . . . People were scared to share their ideas and a book . . . would help people feel at ease.*

This book is intended to give you that background knowledge, and so help you start your creative writing course with confidence, and to help you feel at ease from the earliest stages. It not only explains *what* you will be asked to do but also *why* you are asked to do it.

Doing Creative Writing tells you what to expect in terms of:

- the various elements that are involved in 'doing creative writing';
- what you have to do both in classes and in your own time;
- common course structures and teaching methods;
- common forms of assessment, and the related issues of assessment criteria;
- your fellow students and their possible reasons for doing the course;
- your tutors and their possible reasons for teaching the course;
- your future career.

It also aims to contextualise creative writing as a subject both within the university and in relation to the outside world, and so give you confidence to find your own way and thereby get what *you* want from your course.

What's in this book

Doing Creative Writing is divided into three main parts. The first part outlines the *context* of creative writing as a subject to be taught and learned, and goes on to cover its relatively recent appearance and subsequent rapid growth in universities and colleges. This section also deals with the (sometimes bewildering) variety of places you can find creative writing courses within institutional frameworks, and profiles the kinds of people who study and teach on these courses.

The second part covers the *courses* themselves, their structure, content and how they are taught. Every course is different, but most share certain features in structure and teaching methods so it's possible to outline the ways in which courses are divided up, and the common pathways through them. This part deals extensively with the most widespread form of delivery for creative writing, the *workshop*, telling you what kind of things you may be asked to do, and why, and also gives an idea of how much work you might be expected to do on your own outside of the workshop. This section concludes with a discussion of the kinds of assessment you might encounter, and pays particular attention to 'non-creative', reflective elements of assessment that may appear in your courses as, for example, commentaries, rationales or journals.

The third part deals with the *skills* you should expect to develop throughout the course, including the self-discipline essential to make use of self-directed time, note-taking, organisation and development of ideas, reading as a writer, and the different kinds and levels of editing you'll need to do at different stages of a writing project. This section also deals with the (sometimes undervalued) areas of layout and presentation.

A concluding section deals with possibilities *beyond the course*, covering further study, the skills needed to sell yourself and your work, ways to keep on writing and other careers for which a degree involving creative writing will qualify you. It includes eight representative case studies showing how different people have moved on after having 'done' creative writing. At the end of the book you'll find a section containing suggestions for further reading organised around the topics dealt with in the book.

The book is arranged to help you at each stage of the process of doing creative writing: deciding whether to do it or not; choosing a suitable course; what to expect when you arrive; understanding the structure of your course; how to organise yourself; assessment; progression through the levels of the course; and possibilities after the course. However, 'reading as a writer', you may prefer to use the contents or the index to find the particular topic that interests you at any given time.

PART I

THE CONTEXT

Creative writing: can it be taught?

- Can I learn how to be a better writer?
- Isn't writing more about inspiration than skills that can be taught?
- What do I have to do to improve my writing?

I suppose in other creative disciplines you have to learn how to use all the equipment but [doing creative writing] you don't really have any equipment apart from a pen. (*Student comment*)

I can only write when I'm inspired. (*Student comment*)

The execution belongs to the author alone; it is what is most personal to him, and we measure him by that ... His manner is his secret, not necessarily a deliberate one. He cannot disclose it, as a general thing, if he would; he would be at a loss to teach it to others ... the literary artist would be obliged to say to his pupil ..., 'Ah, well, you must do it as you can!' (Henry James, 'The Art of Fiction')

One of the questions that may be in your mind when considering or beginning a course is whether creative writing can really be taught. You might even be wondering whether a course could interfere with your natural creativity, by imposing rigid methodological frameworks on a process that has always been spontaneous for you. This chapter will argue that to get better as a writer you have to practise, that you have to practise the right things, and that it makes sense to get advice about what to practise from someone who understands how to write well.

Practice makes perfect – or does it?

If you wanted to play the clarinet, you wouldn't expect to pick the instrument up and play it fluently straightaway. You would expect to have to practise. You might also consider it desirable to have instruction, from a book or a teacher.

Why should it be any different for a writer? Because writers have no instrument, other than the pen or word processor, it is often assumed that they are not artists in the same way that musicians or painters or even dancers are.

If we pick up the clarinet for the first time, most of us will be aware of the difficulties awaiting us: we can see the silver levers and buttons, feel the keys under our fingers, the reed rough on our lips. This is by no means a simple piece of kit. No such warnings flash up when we first pick up a pen to write creatively. Not everyone knows how to play a clarinet or use a paintbrush, but everyone knows (or thinks they know) how to use a pen. What's so special about a writer? They're just doing something that anyone can do.

This attitude tends towards the conclusion that if you want to be a writer you don't have to practise, you just wait for inspiration. All that matters for the writer, following this line of thought, is the *idea*. It is assumed that the idea will come complete with the means and form of its expression.

This attitude is not uncommon among students starting to do creative writing, who may insist they can only write when they're inspired. Further, when invited to take part in an exercise, for example to do with story analysis or narrative structure, many students will announce with something approaching pride that they 'never plan'. This is, I contend, something like the learner clarinettist announcing that they can't play a scale, and expecting congratulation.

It is one of my assumptions in writing this book that, in fact, those levers, rods, pads, keys and reeds (or their metaphorical equivalents) are attached to every pen. The fact that they are invisible may lure us in with a false confidence, which wouldn't be such a bad thing if it weren't so quickly dispelled by our early attempts.

When our clarinet squawks or refuses to speak at all, we have a pretty good and visible idea why. When our pen fails to produce the poetry that glowed in our head, it's easy to get discouraged. As one student put it: 'I've got a head full of good ideas, but every time I write one down it comes out ordinary'.

Poet Ted Hughes makes a similar point in his book *Poetry in the Making*:

> When I was young, I was plagued by the idea that I really had much better thoughts than I could ever get into words.

This dissatisfaction is probably not due to the *idea* being poor but to the writer trying to play the concerto before mastering the instrument.

So if you are tempted to protest, when asked to try a certain exercise or approach, 'I never do that', or 'I can't do that', reflect on the clarinet parallel. No, you don't do that, no you can't do that, but it is the business of your course to *teach* you how to do it. But I'm running ahead of myself. We're nowhere near enrolling on a course yet.

It is the contention of this book that for someone to write well without practice (leave aside instruction for the moment) is as likely as someone picking up a brush for the first time and painting the *Mona Lisa*, or picking up a clarinet for the first time and sailing through a Mozart concerto, or, for that matter, picking up a golf club and winning a major championship. They may know what they want the picture to look like, they may know what the music ought to sound like, they may even be able to clout the ball a fair distance, but they will need to do a lot of work on all kinds of aspects of technique before they have any chance of realising what they have imagined.

Now, you might well say, pretty well all of us have some writing skills, learned at school and elsewhere – certainly more writing skills than we have clarinet-playing skills. Surely this puts us in a better position than our first-time painter or clarinettist. Very well, to make the analogy fairer and closer to the truth, let us allow our would-be *Mona Lisa* painter some experience in interior decoration and the creosoting of fences, and give our clarinettist an apprenticeship on the swannee whistle. Relevant experience, but not adequate, and that is the position of most of us in terms of writing skills when we first try to write creatively.

To sum up: it is a central assumption of this book that if we want to improve and become effective writers, we must work, and practise. If you don't agree with this, if you feel all you have to do is wait for that flash of inspiration and then start writing, then maybe you should stop reading now and slip this book quietly back onto the bookshop shelf, or (if you've already bought it) try and sell it on eBay. You should also think very carefully about the wisdom of enrolling on a creative writing course.

So (if you're still here) we agree that to improve our writing we have to practise, or at least that the idea of practice is worth considering. But why take a course when you can write perfectly well in your spare time? All you need to do is to write in the privacy of your own home. Practice makes perfect – or does it?

Pressing the brake to go faster

Gary Player, the famous and very successful golfer, when an opponent accused him of being lucky, replied, 'It's funny but the more I practise the luckier I get'. As I've argued above, it's fair to say that you'll have to be very lucky indeed to write anything worthwhile without a lot of practice. However, as my trumpet teacher used to say, it is a fallacy that practice makes perfect, because if you practise doing something the wrong way, bad habits will simply become ingrained and we'll get better at doing it wrong. So, for example, if you practise pressing the brake pedal in order to make your car accelerate, no matter how 'good' you get at pressing the brake pedal, no amount of repetition will increase the speed at which you are travelling.

When I was in my teens, I learned one of Mozart's piano concertos off-by-heart (nearly). I couldn't read music fluently, and I couldn't play anything else on the piano; I just worked out the notes painstakingly slowly, and then played them over and over again (ask the neighbours) until I could play quite a lot of the piece at nearly the proper speed.

A worthy investment of time? Perhaps, if you want a party piece to try and impress people, but in terms of learning, virtually useless, and extremely labour intensive. Why? I was studying one piece of music as though it was unique and had no connection to other pieces of music. Learning to play it did not help me to play any other piece. I couldn't transfer what I'd learned and apply it in a new context.

So, how are you to know what is worthwhile practice and what is the equivalent of pressing the brake pedal? You may have spotted the direction in which my argument is moving. We have established that practice is essential, as is knowing how and what to practise.

Going back to my experiences as a pianist, after taking lessons from an experienced player (and buying an instruction book) I came to recognise common features and generic skills (scales, chords, fingering patterns, for example) that can be used in piece after piece. There are also conventions and principles that underlie musical compositions, which supply context and act as short cuts to understanding how the piece should be performed. Thereby, learning one technique is not a closed end in itself, it is a gateway to other pieces. Now, every time I stumble through one piece, it is easier for me to stumble through a whole lot of other pieces also.

So, might it not also be a good idea for someone learning to write to consult someone with knowledge and experience of the writing process? It seems so logical that I'm almost tempted to rest my case, but there still remains an entrenched belief among many that the teaching of writing is impossible and that writers cannot (or should not) explain their processes.

Heather Leach, in the useful and inspirational *Road to Somewhere*, says: 'It's probably true that no one can *teach* you to become a writer' (p.11). Fiona Mountford, in the *Daily Telegraph* (17 November 2003), concludes a very positive article about a writing course she attended on the following negative note: 'But can people really be taught how to write? The question niggled me. The obvious answer is no'.

Why is that answer obvious? Common sense would seem to point in the opposite direction. If you can teach painters and musicians and dancers, why can't you teach writers? Why is writing a special case? Novelist Henry James, in 'The Art of Fiction', explains as follows:

> The painter *is* able to teach the rudiments of his practice ... If there are exact sciences there are also exact arts, and the grammar of painting is so much more definite [than that of writing] that it makes the difference.

According to James, then, you *do* need to practise, but you can't be *taught* very much by someone else, because every piece of achieved writing is unique and made in a unique way. He sees in writing few, if any, parallels with the painter's vanishing point, perspective, composition and light and shade, nor with the scales, chords and fingering patterns of the pianist.

His argument is that while a painter uses the same techniques for every picture, for the writer every project is utterly unique, a new adventure, a journey into the unknown. Therefore, the writer who has written, who has made this journey into the unknown, can be of little or no use to anyone planning to make their own journey, because every journey has a different and unique destination. The aspiring writer must learn to write in the same way as I learned my first Mozart concerto, in a lonely, blind struggle along an unmapped route where not even one's own experience is of any use in understanding the process.

If this is the case, then the teaching of writing is impossible, and signing up for a course in creative writing is a waste of your time and that of your teachers. To quote James again: 'The literary artist would be obliged to say to his pupil . . ., "Ah, well, you must do it as you can!" '

No-one in their right mind is going to cough up good money for that kind of advice. But is James right? The fundamental point at issue would seem to be the existence, or not, of (to use James's own word) a 'grammar'; that is, common features shared by different pieces of writing, like the chords, scales and rhythmic patterns of music.

Do various pieces of writing share common features? On the face of it, surely yes, at every level. We don't have to invent a new language every time we write or speak; we use conventions of grammar and punctuation. At the level of meaning we each have our differing but related take on the shared pool (see 'Authors, dead or alive' below, p. 22). If I say 'boat', you will probably conceive of something boat-like, not something mountain-like or goat-like (unless you misheard me). At the level of narrative, can't we discern classes of point-of-view (some books use first person, some third etc.), and don't all stories share basic patterns, however complex, beautiful or convoluted the telling (someone wants something and tries to get it in the face of difficulties)?

We will return to these shared features in Part 3 of this book, but, for the time being, we can (I hope) agree that they exist and that they are recognisable, and hence capable of definition and being passed on from one person to another. To take one simple example: I can show you models of basic story structure (that is teaching), and you can apply one of those models to your own ideas (learning).

IN PRACTICE

You want to write a story. I don't know what your story is about, what genre you want to write in, or anything else about it. However, because (I believe) stories share common features, I can be fairly certain that if you ask yourself the following questions about your story, it will help you to discover its shape and point:

1. Who is it about?
2. How do they change over the course of the story?
3. What do they want?
4. Do they get what they want?
5. Who (or what) is trying to stop them?
6. What are the key events in the story?
7. Which event decides whether the main character gets or doesn't get what they want?
8. How does it end?
9. Which other characters are *absolutely essential* to the story?
10. Where is the best place to start?

Can Henry James (or anyone else for that matter) deny this simple proposition? Probably not. And I wouldn't have spent so long on this argument were not the hangover from it still apparent in the teaching and learning of creative writing today.

Now, if you are a student in the United States, at virtually any level, taking a compulsory Rhetoric or Composition programme, or a student of English Language in the UK, or if you work for a company that believes in the importance of writing skills, or if you are involved in the teaching of English as a Foreign Language, or if you are studying science at, say, Warwick University in the UK, you may well have been frowning in puzzlement for some time now and wondering what all this fuss is about.

In all those contexts writing is routinely and, presumably, successfully taught (or why would so many people invest so much time and money in the process?). If you search for books about the teaching of writing outside of the strictly 'creative' area, you'll find titles such as *Strategies for Successful Writing: A Rhetoric, Research Guide, Reader and*

Handbook, or *The Simon and Schuster Handbook for Writers*, which (according to its own publicity):

> explains the purposes of writing, aids in the understanding of grammar, sentence structure, punctuation, gives the processes of research writing, and provides a section for ESL students . . . An excellent reference book for writers, those studying for an English CLEP, or to help all grade levels with English.

What can James and his adherents say to this? Isn't this the teaching of writing, writ large? (The book quoted above is over 900 pages long!)

There must be something else at the root of his argument, something not clearly stated. It would seem to be this (and here I apologise in advance to Henry James for over-simplification): the Jamesian view refers not to techniques of writing but to content. When he refers to 'grammar' he isn't referring to grammar as we know it but a meta-grammar on an aesthetic level. So, you may be able to teach someone (ordinary) grammar, syntax, punctuation, narrative structure, sentence structure, rhythm and descriptive techniques, but (aha, the romantic catch) you can't give them the inspiration, the idea or the essence of the piece of work.

Again, I'm almost tempted to rest my case, so absurd does this argument appear. The proposition seems to be, first, that learning (ordinary) grammar, syntax, punctuation, narrative structure, sentence structure, rhythm and descriptive techniques won't help you with 'creative' writing, but in addition that learning these things (or reflecting on them) will actually harm you as a 'creative' writer.

In this view, the artist is involved in a mysterious process that he or she can neither explain nor pass on. Any kind of analysis of process or explanation of method is to be avoided if not condemned; even to attempt such analysis risks driving out the mystery of the sacred art. The shared features of writing are ignored or looked down on; all attention is focused on the product as a finished, perfect entity; mystical, inexplicable content divorced from technique.

And here we come almost full circle: we have met two constituencies who seem to be embracing 'inspiration' as the essence of creative writing. At one extreme the high priest Henry James, anxious not to sully or spoil his mystery with analysis, and at the other the novice who doesn't relish the prospect of the hard work involved in learning their 'instrument'. Of course, James is not advocating lack of work, far from it. He is suggesting that all writers should tackle each project like the misguided young pianist whose approach means that every piece is an entirely new and mysterious challenge, nothing learned from the previous experience either of self or others. For him, the process is arduous, but mystical and inexplicable; the 'inspiration'-dependent novice likes the mystic but misses out the hard work altogether. And so we sometimes find inexperienced writers waiting (patiently or impatiently) for the muse to deliver magnificent finished product on the blank page without their stir.

Perhaps we are now approaching the key to the conundrum. The underlying assumption in the can't-teach camp seems to be that there is a difference in kind between creative and all other ('ordinary') forms of writing.

Perhaps this attitude contributes to the lack of confidence felt by many would-be writers embarking on a creative writing course. One of our case studies says: 'Even after I'd finished the degree, a writer was always someone else, never me'. I can empathise strongly with this feeling. When I was at school and university I felt that writing was something sacred and other, that other people did, special people very different from me. More to the point, I had no conception of the process by which a book is made (and, of course, if James had his way no-one would ever find out except by personal trial and error – and then be unable to share the knowledge).

One of the purposes of any creative writing course is to make the student feel confident enough to see him/herself as a writer, whether or not he/she eventually succeeds in getting published. Romantic and mysterious attitudes, which turn writers (once successful, preferably in a certain limited 'literary' genre) into an unapproachable priesthood, do not help with this progression; indeed they serve to deter some people from even setting a foot on the lowermost rung of the ladder.

I am going to suggest an alternative reading of 'mystery', one that involves hard work and well-directed practice, but which does not demand membership of any secret society. One element of this argument is that all forms of writing are related, that creative writing isn't a lone, unique and special case.

Craft and mystery

You may have heard of the medieval 'mystery' plays, plays based on the biblical stories of the Old Testament and the life and death of Jesus. They are called 'mystery' plays not because there's anything mysterious about them but because they were produced by the 'mysteries' or craft guilds, the Shipwrights, the Tanners or the Stonemasons. These guilds were called mysteries because those practising them knew the secrets of their respective crafts. It might be more useful to think of creative writing as being 'mysterious' in this sense.

Some teachers of creative writing get a little uneasy when the word 'craft' is mentioned, and they may mutter darkly about the horrors of 'professional' writing courses that force writers into the straitjacket of an imposed, sterile correctness. They resist the reduction of art to craft and argue that an emphasis on technique rather than inspiration thwarts creativity.

I can only go back to the musical analogy. It is true that a musician may have superb technique but be unmusical in performance; like my piano tuner, who knows only one piece of music and plays it (relentlessly) throughout the tuning process simply in order to determine the progress of his tuning. As music, the piece is flashy and (perfect), but strangely unmusical, lacking something, though what it is that it lacks is hard to define. However, that's a special case and probably on a par with my own Mozart-learning experience. The music academies don't relentlessly churn out a stream of unmusical, one-piece automatons. Being able to play your instrument doesn't debar you from musicality. On the contrary, we can say with certainty that no musician *without* technique will be able to do justice to (say) a Mozart concerto. Learning the physical techniques of the instrument will make the player aware of certain constraints – for example, in the case of our clarinettist, the normal range of the instrument, that is how high or how low they can play. Is it a bad thing for the player to be aware of these constraints? Of course not. Only when the player understands the rules and limitations of their instrument can they make an informed decision either to stay within those limits or try, by whatever means, to overcome or transcend them. Simply dreaming of heavenly sounds will not make untutored, unpractised squawking sound any better.

Of course in fiction and poetry as in music we value the original, the complex and, yes, we want to produce magical and mysterious responses in our readers. But I would maintain that we are, in this sense, like professional illusionists rather than 'real' magicians. We achieve our impressive effects not by mysterious powers but by a set of tricks, deceptions, wires, mirrors, smoke and, above all, practice in sleight of hand, the palming of coins and concealment of rabbits. No magician will manage a convincing trick just by picking up a pack of cards and hoping for the best; and we'll sit a long time beside an empty top hat waiting for a rabbit to appear, no matter what spells we utter. Nor will we produce convincing creative writing by doing the same with our pen and a blank sheet of paper.

There is another important point here. To perfect the card trick we must practise, and *must be prepared to get it wrong*. It is perhaps the most dangerous implication of the James approach that we will be discouraged from getting it wrong, from 'making a mess'. We see finished perfection, we attempt to imitate the same and when we produce something less than perfect we give up. And that is the worst possible result.

To conclude, it must be a fundamental belief for anyone teaching or doing creative writing that Henry James is wrong; that writers' journeys share common features, even though some be in lands of sand and some in snow, and that there are skills and techniques to be learned that have a wider application than the one-off, unique work. Every book or play or poem is different, but there are principles, structures and techniques underlying this variety that are held in common.

We have, I hope, agreed that in order to write well you must practise, and that it's no bad thing to get guidance from those who have experience of writing and who have reflected on the process. Why not, then, do creative writing?

But, just a moment, you don't have to 'do' creative writing at university in order to get guidance from writers; there are all kinds of writing courses available, aren't there? Indeed there are, and so in the next chapter we will examine what makes doing creative writing at university different.

Summary

- To get better at anything you have to practise.
- You also have to do the right kind of practice.
- It makes sense to get advice from someone who is good at the thing you're practising.

IN PRACTICE

1. How regularly do you write? Try this exercise. Starting from now, work backwards for exactly one week, noting down what writing you've done, and when. Don't just include 'creative' writing; note everything – shopping lists, academic essays, e-mails to your bank manager, even forms and lottery tickets. Can you see any patterns? More important, can you see any gaps, any opportunities that you're missing?

2. Try keeping a diary. In my experience you will probably have to set aside a certain time of day to do this, maybe either first thing in the morning or last thing at night. When you write, keep asking yourself the following questions:

    (a) For whom are you writing? (Are you imagining a perfect 'listener' or someone you know?)

    (b) Would you write differently if you knew someone (your mother, your tutor, your partner) was going to read it?

    (c) Are you simplifying events? Is it too tedious and complicated to try to explain every in and out of the catflap?
         [Here's the tough one:]

    (d) Are you lying to yourself? Are you making excuses, or smoothing over awkward moments, or attributing motivations that perhaps might not have pertained at the time of the incidents you are recording?

    (e) For a little light relief and change of perspective, try writing the diary in the third person ('he' or 'she' instead of 'I'). Does it read back like a story/novel? If not, why not?

2

Creative writing: why take a university course?

- What makes a university course different from other courses?
- What will I have to do apart from writing?
- Why do I have to read other writers?
- What might the benefits of a formal creative writing course be?

There is a long history of writing courses outside of higher education. These range from those correspondence courses you may have seen advertised in some newspapers, which promise to refund your money if you don't earn it back from selling your writing, through week-long or weekend residential courses (such as those run by the Arvon Foundation), to evening classes and writing groups that are avowedly for 'fun', treating writing as a hobby rather than for success or profit.

Undergraduate creative writing courses are rather different from all of these. It is the purpose of this book as a whole to explore why in some detail, but this chapter will look at the basic distinguishing features in order to begin to give you an idea of what to expect when doing creative writing.

A course is a course, isn't it? What makes a degree course different

In all undergraduate creative writing courses there must be some element of *level* and some element of *progression*. To take a UK example, in the case of a single unit or module in an English degree, the standard of work must in some way be consistently comparable to other (non-creative writing) modules in that degree. In the case of a three-year Single Honours creative writing programme, the whole must be consistent, with equivalent standards being set at each of the three levels, and with progression between the levels. Also, the degree as a whole must be of a comparable standard of difficulty and achievement to any other degree programme, whether it be English, History or Biology.

US institutions of higher education also follow a similar model. Once a student has decided to focus on writing, either through a major (like a first), or a minor, or an emphasis, they progress through a series of levels. These begin, typically, with a beginning, multigenre exploration of the field, often titled 'Introduction to Creative Writing', then move on to intermediate and advanced courses that emphasise certain genres and often conclude with intensive, senior-level capstone courses. This progression is, of course, modelled on majors and minors in other fields, which are intended to move a student from an introductory level to an advanced mastery of a subject.

Put simply, this not only means that you should get better at writing as you go along, but also that you should know more and understand more. Although there are differing methods of monitoring these aspects in the US and Australia, the same is generally the case there too.

By contrast, if you join a writers' group, with open entrance and no assessment, you will probably find a huge range of talent, ability and ambition – and it doesn't matter. Such groups can be mutually supportive, and all participants can get satisfaction regardless of how well they do and what progress they make. Let me offer an extreme example. When I used to run a creative writing group in a prison there were several very talented writers. There were also a couple who came purely to break their routine, and one who couldn't actually read or write at all. When he managed to write the sentence 'My name is XXXXX', the sense of achievement he got (and the rest of us vicariously for him) was the same as if someone had published a novel. The same couldn't happen in an undergraduate context because there are official standards that anyone who successfully completes a degree programme should achieve, whatever the field of study. In the UK these are known as *outcomes* and are laid down by the Quality Assurance Agency (QAA) for higher education, a national, government-monitored organisation. We need not go too deeply into these outcomes here, but they include such things as 'a systematic understanding of key aspects of their field of study' and 'the ability to manage their own learning'.

The QAA also demands a rigorous process of *validation*. Before any course is offered at a university it has to be assessed by experts both within and outside the institution to ensure that the programme is of an appropriate level and fit for purpose. In non-UK contexts, the processes are somewhat different, but you can be sure that any university course you consider will be monitored by somebody other than your tutor to ensure that it is meeting certain criteria along the lines of those set in the UK.

So, learning to write one's own name will probably not meet the requirements of the QAA, university or any other monitoring body. But that's not all. The QAA requirements mean that a degree cannot simply be vocational, in the sense of just teaching you to *do* something. But isn't that exactly why you're doing Creative Writing – learning to write novels or poems or plays? A Creative Writing degree may appear to be vocational, in a way that, say, a History degree isn't. This is misleading. Not every graduate of a Creative Writing degree will become a published writer. Even fewer will earn a living from writing, and, to put it baldly, say you are talented or lucky enough to get published while on the course, you will be happy, and your tutors will be happy, but in order to get your degree you have to do more than just produce work of publishable quality; you have to *reflect* on what you write and *put it in context*. And if your published work doesn't conform to the assessment criteria of the course you're taking, you won't pass the course either.

We will talk more of these requirements and the thinking behind them in Part 2 of this book. For now, the vocationality issue brings us to the very pertinent (and perhaps personal) question of why you are doing, or thinking of doing, a degree that includes creative writing.

My own research suggests that it is very likely that you are thinking of doing Creative Writing not just because you want to be a writer (if that's what you want) but also because you want a degree (see 'Who's doing creative writing' in Chapter 3, p.44). And if that's the case, it means you will be expected to do more than if you were simply taking a course with publication (or personal pleasure) in mind. If publication is your only concern, or if you just want to write as a hobby, then you might like to consider some of the other options outlined above.

Doing creative writing, then, broadly speaking, involves two elements: learning how to write, and reflecting on that learning. Not every successful writer in the 'real' world engages in the second, reflective activity. As we have already seen, some writers think such reflection unhelpful or impossible. This reluctance might, to some extent, account for 'second novel' syndrome – the difficulty many writers have in completing a second novel, where the first has been instinctive and heartfelt.

Here we can conclude that doing creative writing at university level is a much broader education than attending other kinds of writing classes. We might say that in order to complete a course successfully you must: know what others have done before and elsewhere; have the conceptual skills to plan something of your own; have the executive skills to make that thing; and have the analytical skills to understand and contextualise what you have done.

Now let's look more closely at these other activities, activities outside of the actual writing.

Process and product: authors, dead or alive

> I don't know how I wrote it, I just wrote it. (*Student comment on their own writing*)

Another way of thinking about this idea of writing and reflection is to consider the concepts of *process* and *product*. It is easy to assume that many forms of writing we encounter every day 'wrote themselves': for example, mundane items like instruction manuals or fire drill notices. However, it is salutary to remember that each and every one of these was written by a writer who had to go through a more or less complex process in order to achieve the finished product.

If you don't believe me or if you think producing a piece of functional writing is easy, try what might seem a relatively simple task – writing instructions for how to get to your home. Immediately you are faced with a whole set of preliminary questions before you can put pen to paper: Who is the instruction for? Where are they coming from? By what means of transport? How much can you assume that they know (can you say 'come off such-and-such a road at such-and-such a junction', or do you have to describe how to find that initial road?). And how much research do you need to do in terms of train and bus routes and schedules? In other words, you will be forced to engage in a whole variety of activities *outside of the actual act of writing*. If you were to record those activities, how you went about doing them and what results and conclusions you came to, you would have a record of your *writing process*.

What has this to do with writing a high-art, literary novel, or any kind of novel, poem or play?

I would argue that it is, similarly, very easy to look on published works (especially 'classics') purely as finished objects, which have descended fully formed and perfect to the library shelves. While we may view the guidebook directions as unworthy of a human author, we may (especially if we have any residue of the Henry James' romantic mystery about us) view the classic literary masterpiece as transcending mere mortal process.

This concentration on *product* rather than *process* (apparently and perhaps superficially) would seem to draw support from literary criticism and critical theory. For example, the well-known work of French writer and critic Roland Barthes notoriously proclaims 'The death of the author'. Barthes' contention (put over-simply) is that the author is irrelevant to the piece of writing. The writing creates and partakes of its own context and meaning, depending on its reader and his/her experience, and therefore for all useful intents and purposes the writer is 'dead'.

The insidious implication of the 'death of the author' is that because texts are self-sufficient, independent of the writer, then the writer's intentions and efforts are irrelevant, and therefore, some might conclude, superfluous – which leads us neatly back to the hopeful clarinettist sitting waiting for a Mozart concerto to emerge from the end of his instrument.

The efforts and intentions of the writer may well be irrelevant to the reader after the book is written, or at least published and read. However, books don't (yet) make themselves. They can't replicate without human intervention. Even if you buy a plagiarised piece over the internet, someone wrote it. Put baldly, the fact is that most if not all authors are indisputably alive, at least while writing. As a writer, and as a student of creative writing, you are necessarily and immediately concerned with live authors – yourself, your fellow students and those writers of works you admire, despise or wish to understand and emulate.

And here we arrive at another fundamental feature of Creative Writing: if you do Creative Writing you are concerned primarily with the process by which work is made, and that process necessarily involves a live author, thinking, experimenting and making tactical and strategic decisions. This focus on *process* rather than *product* is one key factor that distinguishes Creative Writing from the traditional study of English literature.

Traditional English tends to look for effects in literature, it doesn't (much) concern itself with how those effects are achieved. To give a simple example, the literary critic might say that a poet writing the line 'Peter Piper picked a peck of pickled peppers' has 'used alliteration'. This analysis, however accurate and insightful for readers, gives little or no insight into the process by which the line actually was written, or how we as writers might use alliteration profitably ourselves. Did the p's come first or the peppers? Did the character have a name or did the name follow the alliteration? Did the writer try it with a different sound first (Charles Chaney chose a chaldron of chunky cheese chutney)?

Similarly, some critics might be interested in what James Joyce was up to during the 20-year composition of *Finnegan's Wake* for cultural or sociological reasons, or for parallels between his life and his art. As writers we are interested in how his working practices can shed light on techniques of composition that we can adopt, reject or modify for ourselves.

The distinction between process and product is rather like the difference between the attitudes of a clock maker and connoisseur-owner to a fine old clock. The owner admires it, reveres it, perhaps criticises it if it doesn't keep perfect time, maybe researches its history, and also uses it. The clock maker will strip it to its essentials in order to learn how it works. This analogy is especially apt because this deconstruction will not be purely mechanical. The clock maker will want to understand not only how the mechanism works but also how the fine case, face and the rest is made and integrated into a whole.

So, back to instruction manuals and high-art literature. Now, I would argue (though some teachers of creative writing would not agree) that we should treat all kinds of writing as differing manifestations of the same process: that we can learn from studying how a fire notice gets written just as we can learn from studying James Joyce's writing processes. The fact that writing any kind of creative work is of a higher order of complexity than (say) writing an instruction for a guidebook only strengthens this argument. Reflecting on the process we go through to write the guidebook entry gives us a clear picture of the kind of process we're going to have to go through in writing our piece of literature – clear because stripped bare of distracting questions of 'originality' and 'mystery' that the creative work brings with it.

First and foremost, as writers of travel instructions or novels, we must think about our audience – who are we writing for and why? You may be tempted to answer (many writers do), 'I don't know who I'm writing for, I just write'. Fair enough, and it may be (like a blind archer) that you hit your target without knowing what that target was or where it was standing. However, you won't do very well on a degree-level creative writing course, which as we have seen demands contextualisation and consideration of process.

And while it may not be necessary to research train times and schedules for your novel (you can make them up), there are a myriad other things which, even if you make them up, you will have to understand fully and make consistent (for example characters' ages and life histories, and on a more complex level, their 'off-stage' relationships).

The main thing to realise is that the actual putting of pen to paper, finger to keyboard, is not in itself even the major component of the writing process. That act is like the visible appearance of a complete car at the end of a (largely invisible) production line. Doing Creative Writing involves exploring all the different hammerings and screwings that take place in the heart of the factory.

Whatever we think about the relation of a fire notice and *Ulysses*, the important conclusion here is that without a lot of work and thought *outside of the actual act of writing itself*, it is unlikely, if not impossible, that you will write well, that you will create a self-consistent and convincing world, whatever that world may be. We will talk about this work outside the act of writing more in Part 3, but for the moment we can at least say that it will probably involve some kind of reflection, research and planning, whether conscious or unconscious.

In case I have given the impression that I regard writing as an exact science, and the writer as the all-powerful captain of a smooth-steaming vessel, I must swiftly haul down the sail and row back (and yes, this metaphor is intentionally mixed).

Writer, reader and reality

Having stressed the importance of the live author for those doing creative writing, it's necessary immediately to make some qualifications. While for those of us doing creative writing the author is alive, he or she is not infallible and omnipotent; on the contrary, the author does not and cannot have total control over his/her work, especially once it gets out into the world. Your work will mean different things to different people, depending on their cultural or social backgrounds. For example, whether they are reading it in Tonga or Thailand, Belgium or Brazil, today or in a thousand years' time.

Just as readers' perceptions differ, you almost certainly don't know precisely what you mean, or what you're trying to say. If you do, your work may well be rather simple and uninteresting. Central to the relationship of writer and reader is the complexity of resonance on different levels, caused by the flux of shared and unshared experiences. What you should have learned from trying to write the journey instruction earlier is that this complexity is not something you have to strive for, it is a natural consequence of human experience and communication. The difficult thing is to avoid the ambiguities and complexities – hence, for example, the famous inadequacy of white-goods instruction manuals.

IN PRACTICE

For a demonstration of the difficulty, if not impossibility, of achieving absolute clarity and lack of ambiguity in writing instructions, try writing them for one or all of the following:

(a) taking a match out of a matchbox and striking it;

(b) tying your (or someone else's) shoelace;

(c) getting a manually geared car moving in a forward direction.

Difficulties you may encounter are:

- knowing how much prior knowledge to assume;
- knowing where to start in terms of explanation (can you call the lace a lace, or do you have to describe it?);
- trying to find names for precise parts of familiar objects;
- lack of shared knowledge of technical terms;
- establishing 'top' and 'bottom' and which 'end' is which;
- defining the extent of actions (for example, 'open');
- prescribing actions that, although apparently simple, in fact involve precise physical control and what might be termed 'touch' (so, in the case of the

match, just how hard do I have to press, and at what speed do I have to strike it in order to make it ignite?)

You might try and get someone else to follow your instructions, but if it's the third example, please make sure all legal requirements have been satisfied.

One of my most enjoyable and illuminating pedagogical experiences occurred some years ago as a teacher of Simplified English, a version of the language used for instruction manuals for flight mechanics. The rationale behind Simplified English is simple and compelling: mechanics, misled by the ambiguities of old instruction manuals, were making (literally) fatal errors when servicing aircraft. For example, people coming across the instruction 'the bolt is tightened to 40psi' regularly moved on to the next instruction, assuming that the bolt was already thus tightened. Changing the instruction to 'the bolt *will be* tightened' didn't much help; this time the mechanics tended to assume someone else (in the future) would do it. The only thing for it was to change the passive voice ('the bolt is tightened') to active (identifying who is the agent): 'You will tighten the bolt to 40psi' doesn't leave much room for misunderstanding, though the personalisation won't please old-fashioned science teachers. For our purposes the important point is this: even if you know exactly what you want to say, and to whom you want to say it, the very nature of language makes precision devilishly difficult.

Figure 2.1 overleaf shows a simple model of the writer/reader/'reality' relationship. The writer sees a 'thing' and describes it in words. The reader reads the words and so creates a thing in their imagination.

The differing preconceptions, knowledge and experience of the writer and reader make it impossible that the two versions of the 'thing' are the same. Nor, of course, can the perceptions of two different readers be identical.

You can demonstrate this by a simple exercise. Show an object to one group of people; get them to describe it without naming it; let them read their descriptions one by one to another group, which has not seen the object, and whose members then try to draw the images evoked in their minds by the descriptions. Not every person will draw exactly the same thing or shape, and what usually emerges is that the descriptions evoke much more intense and interesting images than the 'reality' when it is

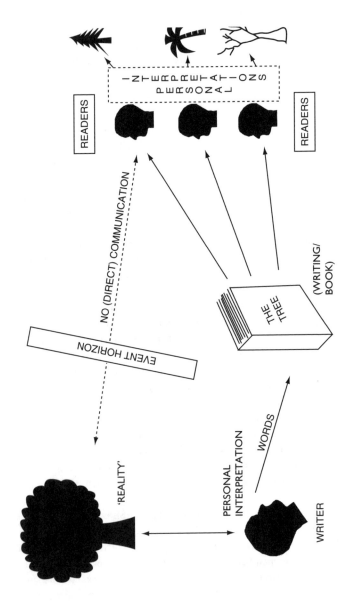

Figure 2.1 A simple model of the writer/reader/'reality' relationship

finally revealed. The most mundane object can be glorified by description. The writer creates 'reality' for the reader – a powerful responsibility; and every created 'reality' is slightly (or widely) different.

When I got a group of graduate students to do this exercise, one of them complained: 'I don't see the point of this, describing things when we don't know what they are'. For me, she summed up precisely the main job of the creative writer: as writers we should approach everything as if we didn't 'know' it. Why? Because if we think we 'know' things, we make assumptions about them, and people. We assume that others share our values and our taste. For writers these assumptions are dangerous, verging on disastrous. If I write my book on the assumption that everyone (like me) eats rotten haddock for breakfast, I'm going to puzzle and lose most people who pick the book up.

IN PRACTICE

Here are three descriptions of everyday objects that are not named. What images do they evoke in your mind?

Mainly blue, hinged at one end, there's a silver plate set into the base and a black tray mounted under the upper arm. A spike juts out behind the hinge.

A grey globe on a white tubular stem. Half-way up the stem there's a black band out of which protrudes a small cream button. The stem rises out of a flat round base. Out of the base snakes a white cord.

Brown and yellow, translucent. The two arms are of equal length, straight until their final downturn. Mounted on the arms are two open ovals joined by a single bridge. The ovals are filled with perspex.

Why not try the same, being as accurate as you can without using any names, and see what images your words evoke in your friends' (or enemies') minds.

Before we conclude, let's revisit Henry James and Roland Barthes, perhaps agreeing to disagree with them both: to Henry James we can say that as authors we may not know *what* we are doing or *why* we are doing it, but we *can* know *how* we did it. To Barthes we can say that the author is alive, but not necessarily conscious or reliable or well-informed. But if you are that writer, and you do seriously set off on the journey, there is no insurmountable pass, no impassable road-block, no phase transition in the quality and humanity of those who write compared with those who don't: there is a continuum from the least accomplished writer to the most celebrated. If we seriously take up the challenge to write, we are all writers.

Summary

When you start doing creative writing you should:

- be prepared to reflect on your practice;
- be prepared to do a lot of work outside of the actual act of writing;
- be aware of the complexity of the relationship between reader, writer and 'reality', and be prepared to question all your assumptions regarding that relationship; and
- take your writing seriously.

Creative writing now

3

- How do I find out about creative writing courses?
- Where do I find creative writing courses?
- What kind of course should I choose?
- Who will teach me?
- How will this affect what I learn and what I do?
- What will my fellow students be like?

This chapter looks at the place of creative writing in universities and colleges, considering both its history and its current status, in order to help you understand the different kinds of courses that are on offer and to get the best out of the course you choose.

Creative writing – where to find it

Creative writing is not always easy to find when browsing prospectuses and websites. Moreover, once you've found a course, it's not always immediately obvious just how much creative writing it contains, or what the purpose of that writing is in the overall context of the course.

In the UK, the Universities and Colleges Admissions Service (UCAS) website is designed as a first port of call for prospective students seeking information on courses nationwide. However, until recently my own institution's courses were listed alongside art and design courses, not under creative writing, presumably because, for historical reasons, their official title was 'Creative Studies in English'.

Similar difficulties can occur with other creative writing courses, because although English is the most common home for creative writing in the UK, not all English courses contain creative writing elements (though the trend is in this direction), and, conversely, creative writing is not confined to English-based courses. In the US, while English departments may house creative writing courses, strictly literature-based courses will contain few creative writing elements, and vice versa for courses in poetry writing, fiction and so forth. As a result, even within the same department these courses are quite separate and usually taught by a different faculty. Moreover, a new trend has emerged in US higher education whereby writing programmes establish themselves separately from English departments in order to pursue their own programmes and major/minor curricula. So in the US, recent figures suggest only 4 per cent of English students enrol for creative writing as opposed to 12 per cent for composition.

In both countries, scriptwriting of one kind or another is often found in Drama, Performance Studies or other media-based courses. It is fairly common for creative writing to be split in this way across an institution, sometimes with little or no formal contact between the script and 'literary' areas. Some journalism or professional writing courses may include creative elements, and creative writing also lives in other more obscure locations like schools of art and design, as at Norwich.

So it is impossible to track all courses that involve or contain creative writing – course and module titles are often opaque in this regard. For example, 'Contemporary Poetry' may or may not include a writing strand.

Creative Writing, even when easily found, is often available in a bewildering variety of combinations. You would be entitled to wonder what a combined degree in biology and creative writing involves; or creative writing and law, or professional and creative writing with sports science, Did someone put those combinations together on purpose, or did they somehow 'just happen'? Do you write about law, or sport? Conversely, do you study the legal aspects of creative writing or are the subjects entirely separate?

All of these factors go to make it difficult for you as a prospective student to find out exactly what's going on and where, and what you will actually be doing if you take creative writing at a particular institution. The only way to understand the range of creative writing on offer in universities, as well as the reasons for this range and, most importantly, how it will affect your studies, is to take brief look at the history of the subject.

The history of creative writing – what's it to you?

In order for you to understand what will be expected of you in a course involving creative writing, it is important to understand how it has developed as an academic discipline. With other, longer established subjects, although there may be arguments about emphasis, there is probably general agreement about what the subject is and why students are doing it. You may be studying law for a variety of purposes, but you would expect all law courses to share common features and give training in certain areas. In contrast, there is as yet no such consensus for creative writing. It is a young subject, having entered the academy within the last 30–40 years in the UK. It has developed in a variety of ways in different institutions and for differing purposes. And what you will be expected to do, and how it will fit in with your degree as a whole, will depend to a great extent on the way the course has developed and why. In the UK there are, broadly speaking, four routes by which creative writing has entered the academy: 1. as an offshoot of English; 2. as an element in theatre, media or other related areas; 3. as a 'practical' element in education courses; and 4. via the expansion of journalism or other 'professional' writing courses.

The situation in Australia and the US is similarly varied, although in the US creative writing has been present in universities and colleges for rather longer (since the 1880s at Harvard, for example). In the US there is the added complication of Rhetoric and Composition as elements in a wide variety of degree-level courses. Creative writing is also increasingly used as a tool around the world for teaching students for whom English is a second language.

In each case creative writing has been introduced because academic staff or institutions have felt it to be a 'good thing', but for different 'good purposes'. The reasons for including creative writing in a course range from the purely academic (in the English context) to the avowedly vocational (journalism and professional writing). If you are doing creative writing as a part of a single module in an English literature degree, the aim will probably be to shed light on the 'real' literature you're studying. By writing a sonnet, you'll understand Shakespeare's sonnets better. There will probably not be much (if any) drive towards publishing your sonnet. At the other extreme, where creative writing has developed from journalism or other professional writing, issues of market will be essential, and you may well expect to be asked to angle your writing towards publication.

Between these extremes, if you are a trainee teacher trying out writing in order to utilise the techniques as part of your own school-teaching repertoire, publication or markets will not be an issue. Experimentation, taking part in exercises and learning how to give useful feedback will be of much greater importance.

If you are studying film, you may not be aiming for Hollywood with your scripts, but knowing how the screenwriting business works will be an essential part of your course, as will learning about proper layouts and terminology. And the trend with film courses is to expand the practical elements, so you may well find yourself learning technical skills to do with cameras and editing as well as scriptwriting.

IN PRACTICE

These four differing views of the aims of good undergraduate creative writing provision come from three different continents and emphasise different aspects, but they should not be taken as nationally specific. You can find programmes with each kind of emphasis in the UK, the US and Australia. Note the wide spectrum, ranging from writing as training for readers to the almost purely vocational, including what might be considered 'non-creative' elements such as corporate writing and publishing.

Students study the interrelationships between literary texts ... Some students may attain this understanding through creative writing.

(UK Draft Benchmark for English)

The goal of an undergraduate program is to teach students how to read critically as writers and to give students the practice of writing frequently so that, by creating their own works, they may apply what they have learned about the elements of literature.

(Association of Writers and Writing Programs 'Hallmarks', USA)

The Fiction Department's goal . . . is to prepare students for a wide variety of careers in creative writing . . . and in jobs where effective communication, creative problem-solving, and group relationship skills are crucial . . . encouraging an understanding of the important connection between aesthetic and professional concerns . . .

(Columbia College, Chicago, Fiction Department
Mission Statement)

This course prepares students to work in creative writing in a range of vocational applications. Subjects covered include fiction, electronic and feature writing, film and TV scriptwriting, non-fiction and youth writing, as well as corporate writing and publishing at both introductory and advanced levels.

(brief description of the Bachelor of Creative Industries [Creative
Writing] course at Queensland University of Technology, Brisbane)

Creative writing within other subjects

Before proceeding I want to digress slightly to talk about why you might find it useful to choose creative writing modules within another subject. To take a concrete example, you are studying drama and the set text is Shakespeare's *King Lear*. Rather than just analysing the text, or even performing the play itself, you are asked to put together a sequence of scenes for a play on a related subject *with the same theatrical and social conditions*. This will involve a practical analysis of:

- cast size;
- cast composition (age and gender);
- size and configuration of the stage;
- expectations of the audience;
- scene structure;
- scene linking; and (of course) finally
- use of language.

So by finding out for yourself the problems and challenges of constructing a scene or sequence of scenes for a play in a particular theatre, you are doing much more than just putting words down on paper. You are (if you do it properly) getting a rich and deep insight into the whole range of processes that underlie the making of a play. You will also get insight into the culture in which that play was performed.

While as a conventional student of English or theatre or drama you are dealing with the finished product, which the writer probably slaved over for a long time in order to make it appear effortless, as a creative writing student you experience at first hand the process of composition and all the effort required to make the product seem effortless.

That experience is certainly worthwhile, and it may be enough for you. In that case creative writing will remain a minor part of your degree, and valuable insofar as it sheds light on your main subject. However, you may wish to take your writing further. In that case you will be better advised to choose a course where the focus, while including study of pre-existing works, has shifted to your own writing.

The growth of creative writing – how it affects your course

What creative writing courses of all kinds share is their growing popularity, which has in turn led to an increase in the number of writing modules or writing opportunities available within various courses. This growth, again, has a direct effect on how you will do creative writing.

If an English department offers an optional 'taster' creative writing element in a single module, it can offer it at any level, and with little thought as to how it fits into the overall pattern of the degree. The writing is isolated and serves purely (in academic terms) to illuminate the core subject.

As soon as more modules or elements are introduced, it becomes essential to think through how the different bits of creative writing relate to each other, and to offer coherent pathways. Piecemeal growth in a modular scheme can lead to a course that offers 'a bit of this and a bit of that', each element self-contained, and the same process being asked of students in each module/course. Therefore, once the number of writing modules available grows beyond a very small number, the questions of coherence and level become increasingly pressing.

For example, if 'writing a sonnet' happened to occur in a second-year module, the question arises, what writing would be appropriate in the first year and the third year? Some courses with limited writing options might split genres by year, so you will do poetry in year one, prose in year two and script in year three. This is only workable when the provision is limited, and even then pedagogical questions arise such as, Which genre is best to study first? Are there skills you learn writing prose that are essential for writing poetry and or vice versa? Why should one genre be level three and another level one? What objective criteria distinguish the work you'll be doing and what you'll be learning?

And if there is to be more than one poetry module (for example, one in each year), what should each contain? Should the split be on the basis of poetic genres (sonnets in year one, ballads in year two and free verse in year three), or should the focus of the course be more on the individual student's taste and development? – so the study of genres is packed in early on, and the later modules are concerned with you as a student finding and refining your own voice in a genre of your choice.

As the provision grows there is a tendency for the focus to shift from using the writing as a tool to illuminate 'real' literature to helping you write well yourself. This in turn will be reflected in the kinds of assessment task you are asked to do (see Chapter 4).

Different institutions have found different solutions to these questions of level and progression. As a prospective student it will be worth your while looking at the shape of a course and asking whether it does just offer 'a bit of this and a bit of that', or whether it offers pathways enabling you to build on what you do at each stage, with a view to producing the very best possible work at the end.

Although, as I've pointed out before, there is as yet no consensus about the content and purposes of a dedicated creative writing degree, most would embrace some version of the Columbia College Mission Statement, which refers to 'the important connection between aesthetic and professional concerns'. It is the balance between 'aesthetic' and 'professional' content and emphasis in courses that it is important for you to understand and gauge as a student.

The situation is complicated because, as creative writing expands in universities, the different kinds of courses and modules mingle, and staff with differing, sometimes competing, interests are required to work together to develop a coherent course and philosophy. It would be dishonest of me to claim that all those involved in the teaching of creative writing share common aims and visions; there *are* tensions, and it is important for you as a student to understand these.

At this point it might be a good idea to meet your potential tutors.

Who's teaching creative writing, and why?

In the US, Australia and the UK creative writing is growing. Provision in the US is said to have quadrupled in the last 20 years. In the UK, recent statistics issued by the English Subject Centre (part of the Higher Education Academy, which is funded by the government and supports the teaching of English literature, language and creative writing in UK higher education) show that creative writing is the fastest-growing element in English university courses. However, it is one of the least common compulsory courses in English departments, but one of the most common optional courses. It is one of the most popular with students but is perceived by academics to have a very low importance.

What do these statistics imply? Creative writing is popular with students; therefore, at institutional level, there is pressure to offer it as an engine for recruitment. However, the majority of English academics do not see it as important. This attitude is reflected in the fact that it is rarely compulsory.

What does this mean for you as a student? It has its main direct effect in terms of who will be teaching you and the power structures within the institution where you study.

It's fair to say that creative writing tutors come to the academy by a greater variety of routes than, say, regular English academics. Some are regular academics with an interest in writing, who may have been published themselves. Others will be practising writers without a formal academic background. And it's worth remembering that the term 'practising writer' covers a variety of people in a variety of situations, ranging from the full-time writer who earns a living primarily from writing, to the occasional writer whose income is earned mainly elsewhere. The basis of the employment varies: some creative writing tutors are permanent full-time members of staff, but many (probably the majority) are employed either on fractional contracts or as part-time, hourly paid lecturers.

To sum up: we might argue that there are four main types of creative writing tutor:

1   those from a conventional academic background (English or some other subject) who have an interest in writing, and may or may not have published creative work themselves;

2   'professional' writers with varying levels of academic qualification and various teaching experience (often employed on fractional contracts or on an hourly paid basis);

3   new academics, who have done creative writing themselves from undergraduate through to Master's or PhD level; and

4   those from a conventional academic background who have been seconded (possibly against their will) by their institution to teach the subject because it will aid recruitment.

There's little to say about those in the fourth category. Clearly, such secondment is bad practice, in principle, and the best you'll get as a student is a more or less adequate, second-hand coverage of the subject delivered without much enthusiasm. In my experience such practice is increasingly rare. I can't offer any fail-safe method for spotting a course that is taught by such tutors, but a quick search of 'Staff' sections on an institution's website can usually give some idea of how experienced in, or committed to, writing tutors are.

In most other subjects those in the third category would predominate; that is people who have studied, say, history at undergraduate level, gone on to do an MA and then doctoral research in the same subject and then found employment teaching the same. This is the usual path for academics in almost all subjects, but because creative writing is so young, such staff are at the moment still somewhat thin on the ground. They represent the future of the subject, because it will be they who define it; by their research, by their course development and by their teaching.

That, however, is for the future. For now, creative writing as a subject is in the same condition as psychology in the mid-nineteenth century; that is, in most cases, in the hands of those not trained within the discipline and with a variety of vested interests. Whereas psychology then had interested parties ranging from medical practitioners to mesmerists, the key to the state and development of creative writing as an academic discipline lies in the interplay between teachers in categories 1 and 2 above.

At one extreme (and I acknowledge an element of caricature in my depiction of these extremes) we find a writer who doesn't have even a first degree, who has never had a 'proper' job (but has done a lot of improper work of various kinds), and who has no clear grasp of higher education and its processes, levels and formal pedagogical and administrative requirements. At the other extreme we have the career academic who has no experience of work outside of academia; to whom the quirks and habits of academia are second nature, who has a passion for writing but no coherent grasp of the process by which a book comes to be written and sold, or of the life of a professional writer. If creative writing is a new element or course in an established department or school it is inevitable that, at least to start with, the latter type (career academics) will be in positions of power, hiring the former (professional writers) to do the work at the 'coal-face'. Such a situation is very common: regular academic staff devising and administering courses actually taught by part-time writer-tutors who are paid only to teach and not to contribute to course development or overall course structure.

You will probably find that with the courses you are considering or taking, you are facing a less extreme example of the scenario I've sketched, but it is still worth finding out who will be shaping and teaching your course. We can then ask how this may affect you as a student.

Writers are, at least by reputation, individualistic and rebellious. Institutions may complain about the difficulty of getting writers to follow the formalities of course delivery. Some have gone so far as to describe writing tutors as 'unreliable troublemakers'. And it's also true that some writers complain of the dead hand of academe stifling their creativity and of the tedium of administration. However, so do many regular academics. I do remember one case where a writer-tutor was so vehemently against the grading of work that he gave all his students 70 per cent. Their success, and his career, were equally short-lived: the work had to be re-marked and he was not offered another contract.

There may well be, all the same, differences of emphasis and expectation between academic tutors and writer-tutors that are worth considering. For example, 'regular' academics may see creative writing as a useful adjunct to their subject, without much intrinsic validity in its own right, while professional writers may tend to over-emphasise the pragmatic and 'vocational' elements (if you're going to write, why not write to sell?). Academic tutors may dislike any or much reference to the market side of writing; they may argue that the academy should be free from the squalid pressures of the commercial world, that students should be encouraged to spread their wings and embark on soaring flights of the imagination.

They also understand the requirements of degree-level study and have certain expectations about student commitment and performance. They know that students want to learn but that they also want a degree.

Writer-tutors, on the other hand, tend to expect a professional level of commitment from students. They imagine that if you're doing a writing course you want to write, and probably want to be a writer. They are surprised if students don't show such commitment. They have a tendency to believe that a student's main aim is (or should be) to produce good, worthwhile writing, without bothering too much about marks, grades or even the degree. As one writer-tutor put it: 'what we're interested in doing is helping people to be good writers, that's it, full stop, that's all we do'.

Is my argument tending towards the conclusion that writer-tutors are the best kind of tutors? Far from it. For a start, not all writers are good teachers.

In Chapter 1 we established that in order to learn how to write you have to do the right kind of practice. We drew the parallel with painting and music, where experienced practitioners pass on their own knowledge of the creative process to others. In order to do this, the practitioner must not only be experienced, but *must also have reflected on that experience*.

Perhaps the worst teachers are 'intuitive' writers, who make a point of not analysing how or why they write what they do. Their best advice is 'be intuitive like me'. For example, when I started teaching writing for radio, even though I had two dozen credits to my name, I didn't have any idea how to do it, because I'd learned to write for radio unconsciously; I'd listened to an enormous number of plays and built up a feel for the way the sounds worked together and the rhythm of scenes and sequences. When building a play I was using an array of techniques but I had never analysed them. Of course, I could have said to my students, 'Go away and listen to radio plays for several years, and then try writing one yourself'. Not bad advice in itself but not very useful in the context of a twelve-week module within a degree programme. So I was forced to analyse what I was doing, to make explicit the questions I was asking of my material, the decisions I was making and the criteria I was applying. I can't be sure if this analysis helped my students, but it certainly helped me.

IN PRACTICE

Here's a hypothetical idea for a play and some basic questions about characters (and other things) that will help the writer find the play's best shape. I
have then added some 'wrong' and some 'right' answers to those questions.

*John is married to Jane. John goes on a trip to Scotland where he
talks about his life to a bishop whom he meets in a fish shop. While
he is away Jane meets an Australian juggler with whom she is tempted
to have an affair. When John comes back he tells Jane all about the
bishop.*

1. What is John and Jane's relationship like at the start of the play?
2. What is the 'trigger' that makes John go to Scotland?
3. What is the significance of the fish shop as a meeting place?
4. What is the function of the bishop: does he just listen, or does he either
    act or incite some action?
5. What is it about the Australian juggler that particularly attracts Jane?
6. How has John and Jane's relationship changed by the end of the
    play?

'Wrong' answers

1. John and Jane's relationship is just normal. [*What on earth do you mean
    by 'normal'?*]
2(a). There was no trigger, it was just a gradual build up of pressure. [*Maybe in
    a novel but not in a play. Plays need events.*]
2(b). He was sent by his employers. [*OK, but you have to think through
    whether he welcomes the break from home or dreads it.*]
3. It actually happened in the fish shop; this is a true story. [*Irrelevant; never
    let the 'truth' spoil a good story.*]
4. The bishop symbolises the Church; he just listens. [*Unless he does or
    provokes something, he's a waste of space: ditch him and find someone
    else for John to meet.*]
5. It doesn't have to be an Australian juggler, it could be anyone. [*This kind
    of minor character should represent (or appear to represent) the desires
    of the major character, Jane. If he doesn't, ditch him and find one who
    does.*]
6. Nothing has changed. [*Then why did you write the play?*]

'Right' answers
1. They pretend all is well, but both harbour secret desires and dissatisfactions.
2. Jane asks John to come with her to the Australian juggling club. He can't bear the idea of all those balls, and so makes an excuse involving a business trip.
3. John is drawn to the fish shop to indulge his lurid and hitherto secret and repressed fish-and-batter fantasies.
4. The (apparently respectable) bishop is in fact a fish-and-batter fantasist on the verge of ruin.
5. The Australian juggler appears to Jane as exotic and liberating, capable of freeing her from John's repressive behaviour.
6. Jane learns that juggling can be a risky business; John that too much fish can be sickening. They return to each other wiser, but don't quite tell each other *everything*.

Again, writers who have achieved success quickly and easily often tend to ascribe this success (perhaps rightly) to their innate personal worth, so their advice boils down to 'Be talented like me'. Perhaps more important, writers who haven't (yet) had to deal with failure or projects that go wrong, may not be the best people to assist you if you have not had success and are wrestling with a piece that won't come out right.

David Morley, head of the prestigious writing programme at Warwick University, once made the following recommendation to anyone employing writing tutors:

> Appoint the hungry, and reward them well. Don't appoint professors, appoint young poor writers who are really keen to impress . . . A lot of writers who are in genres that don't pay much at whatever stage they reach, for instance, poor playwrights, all poets, second-time novelists whose first novels were critical hits but the sales were *glacial*, they're actually quite good teachers because they have learned to sing for their supper, and they know the abyss that waits for them if they do not sing well.

Behind the humour there lie serious points. Although it's far from always the case, professors may be too aloof, or too successful, or just too busy to help someone on the early learning slopes. Writers who have had to struggle both with their work and with earning a living may be much better placed to help you starting out.

And this brings us full circle, because at our other extreme we have the regular academic who is passionate about writing but hasn't published. They can therefore bring a whole range of skills and experience to their teaching that can be of enormous value to the student. For a start, you can hope that they're trained to teach. They will also be trained in critical analysis, so they can spot quickly what's wrong with a piece of writing; they can put writing in context, because of their breadth of reading; and if they are an unpublished novelist they will understand the effort and pain inherent in the process.

In the end, there's no hard and fast rule regarding the 'best' kind of tutor. However, it's important to be aware of the possible differences in approach between different types of tutor. If you've started a course, it can help you avoid confusion; and if you've still to make a choice of course, these considerations may help you do so. If you're at this decision-making stage, and trying to identify the tutors that will help you the most, much obviously depends on what you want from the course. This leads us to the question, 'Why are you doing creative writing?' Can you assume that the other students on your course will be doing it for the same reasons?

So let's take a surreptitious look through the keyhole into the seminar room where your peers are waiting for that first workshop.

Who's doing creative writing, and why?

> I think all the lecturers, spuriously, think that everyone on this course wants to be a writer. (*Student comment*)

Statistics are, of course, notoriously unreliable, but we can draw some general conclusions about the people with whom you will be sharing the seminar room. Official figures in the UK give around a two-to-one majority of women over men for 'Imaginative Writing'; for English the ratio is more like three-to-one, but for journalism the numbers are nearer (though not quite) one-to-one. In the US 56 per cent of all undergraduate students in 2001 were female. In both the UK and US, the age profile of undergraduate students is falling. Fewer mature students are doing creative writing, and the chances are that seven or eight out of ten of your group will either be coming directly from school or will have taken only a year out before starting the course.

Why are they doing creative writing? Of course this depends to a greater or lesser extent on how large a part creative writing plays in their course as a whole. If it is just one small part of the course, you may do it out of curiosity, or even by accident. If it's a large proportion, then clearly your decision must, or should, be based on more strategic considerations.

Surveys at my own institution suggest that around 40 per cent of those doing creative writing want to be professional writers. A similar proportion want to do English, but in a new, different and perhaps more 'personal' way. A large minority are would-be teachers, taking creative writing in order to enhance their teaching. Many mature students are doing it with no practical end in view, because they have come to a point in their lives where they feel they want to do something 'for themselves', and a small minority are what might be termed time-wasters, or free-loaders, who think that creative writing will be a soft option. It is also a fact worth noting that over 80 per cent of students recently surveyed at my institution put 'gaining skills valuable in the market-place' as a high priority in doing creative writing.

So there is no one simple reason for doing creative writing; what is important is that you understand why you want to do it and then make sure the course you're applying for is suitable. Questions to ask, of yourself and of a prospective course are:

- How much creative writing do you want to do?
- Why do you want to do it?
- Are there career implications in certain choices? (For example, if you want to teach in schools in the UK, you probably won't be able to do an English secondary Postgraduate Certificate in Education unless your degree contains 40–50 per cent of 'straight' English or another conventionally recognised subject.)
- How much creative writing does the institution offer?
- Is it offered as practical training to write or as an adjunct to help illuminate another subject?
- Who will be teaching it: are there specialised staff, are they publishing writers, or are they specialists in English or another discipline?

If you've already embarked on your course, it's still worth asking yourself these questions, so that you can be clear about your own motivation, what you need from your course and what you're likely to get at your current institution. Once you're clear about what you want or need, you'll be better equipped to get it, either from your course or by researching other ways of securing the support you need from outside.

Summary

- Creative writing is a relatively young and fast-growing academic discipline.
- This can make it difficult to find where it is offered, and the form in which it is offered.
- It is taught by a wide variety of tutors with a wide variety of interests and agendas.
- Those studying it do so for a variety of reasons.
- Before applying to do creative writing you should understand why you want to do it, what you want out of the course and then find a course that offers what you want.

PART II

STUDYING CREATIVE WRITING

4

How courses are organised and how you will learn

- How much time will I spend studying each week?
- How are the units taught?
- What is a workshop?
- What will I be asked to do?

Choices, units and contact time

You've researched available courses, picked the one that's best for you, got the requisite grades, secured your place and arrived on campus. Each course and institution will have its own content and organisation, and you should look carefully at specific course outlines to find out how you will be taught. One area of common ground in creative writing courses is that you will be expected to attend workshops or seminars, and perhaps lectures and tutorials. Crucially, you'll be expected to complete the bulk of your course requirements outside the scheduled 'contact' hours.

For example, an undergraduate degree in the UK might involve six to ten contact hours per week, but you would also be expected to work independently for around 30 hours in the 26 or so teaching weeks of the year. In the US you would expect more contact time – up to 20 hours per week – but this will probably involve a lot of study outside of your specialist subject area.

This section of the book will look at what you can expect in terms of contact with your tutors and fellow students, while Part 3 will look at working outside the contact hours.

How are creative writing courses taught?

Most courses are split up into units, often called modules. Usually these units will be more or less self-contained, each with its own aims, objectives and assessment items. Some courses are structured so that creative writing units are available at different levels on a 'taster' basis. If you're going to do a course that involves creative writing throughout the programme, you will probably begin with a general compulsory unit with a title like 'Introduction to Creative Writing', 'Starting to Write' or 'General Writing Workshop', which will prepare you for more specialised modules in subsequent years. In the US, this multigenre unit is usually covered in one 13–16-week semester.

By the end of the course you will almost certainly be expected to work independently, for example on a project or dissertation module. Some courses also include modules based on the process of writing, including research and study skills, or elements sometimes known as Personal and Academic Development, which are aimed to help you shape your course towards your future employment opportunities.

The units are usually taught using a mixture of some or all of the following: seminars; workshops; lectures; tutorials; virtual learning environment.

Before talking about these in more detail, a general point needs to be made. Perhaps more than other humanities disciplines, creative writing does not consist of an objective 'store of knowledge' that the tutor can dig up in chunks and pass on to you. If there are two tutors teaching the same unit they will almost certainly differ in the way they teach it, the examples they use and their emphasis. In extreme cases they can disagree, apparently fundamentally, about the best way to approach a particular writing issue. It's one of the key features of doing creative writing as a degree subject that you should approach all issues *critically*. Yes, you should be willing to try different methods and follow different advice, but don't follow uncritically; always ask yourself if a particular technique works for you, and if it doesn't, find out why not.

The situation is complicated because in most (though not all) institutions creative writing will not be taught on a cohort basis. In other words, you won't be meeting the same people each week through the three years of a degree course. Different people will be taking writing in different combinations with other subjects, and there will probably be options within writing, so that you meet different people for different units.

So in a second-year poetry group, for example, not only will there be diversity of ability and motivation but there will also be wide divergence in the amount of creative writing in each individual's degree. Sitting on your left-hand side may be the dedicated would-be writer taking writing modules only, while on your right may be a history student taking creative writing as a minor element of their degree. One of these students (we can't be sure which one) may have done a first-year poetry module and the other may not.

This absence of a common core curriculum is one of the challenges of doing creative writing, both as a student and as a tutor.

Lectures, tutorials and virtual learning environments

As I have mentioned, the common core element of a creative writing course is the workshop or seminar, and I will look at these in some detail. First though, a word about other teaching contexts that you might encounter.

In a **lecture** a tutor delivers a prepared presentation on a given topic such as 'Humour' or 'Narrative Perspective'. Lectures are often used to bring together multiple groups in a plenary, and to give themes for workshop or seminar activity. So after a lecture on humour, you go to your seminar or workshop and try writing humour. Lectures may also be linked to assessment items: therefore failure to know what your lecturer said on a key topic may cost you in terms of grades. As in any other subject it makes sense to take lecture notes and, equally important, keep them in a form that enables you to refer to them.

The **tutorial** is when you get the chance to see your tutor on a one-to-one basis, or occasionally in a small group, to discuss your individual work and progress. The chances are that you will have only very limited time in your tutorial. So, if possible, prepare beforehand. Make a note of any questions you want to ask and any points about which you're unclear or uncertain. Don't go to a tutorial in a passive state of mind, expecting your tutor to make all the running. Remember that your tutor is your primary audience; he or she may also be marking your work during and at the end of the course. In this sense your relationship with your tutor is quite close to that of a professional writer and an editor. Therefore it makes sense to treat these meetings as a chance not only to learn but also to sell yourself and your work. At the very least it can do no harm if your tutor enjoys talking to you.

If you have questions and queries and no scheduled tutorials, most permanent tutors will have 'office hours' when they are available to students. If this is not the case with your tutor, for example if he or she is part-time, track down the member of staff who has overall responsibility for the unit you're taking, often called a 'leader' or 'co-ordinator'.

In the US, lecture and discussion are normally combined in the same class period. The instructor generally comments upon students' work during class time and the amount of one-to-one tutorial time available is at the discretion of the instructor. Tutorials, or one-to-one sessions between student and instructor, are far less common in the US where such practices have not been historically institutionalised.

Virtual learning environments, or VLEs, are designed to be accessible by computer either in institutional IT rooms or from outside the university. VLEs are growing and spreading so it's worth checking before you apply how good an institution's IT support is, especially if you don't have access to a computer or have a computer that can't access the internet. It's increasingly common for halls of residence to have IT facilities that will enable you to 'work from home' rather than having to make a special trip to a communal IT facility.

When a VLE is used it can be a compulsory part of your course, a support for it or a supplement to it. When *compulsory*, there will be exercises that you must complete as part of your assessment. Although these systems are being refined all the time, the kinds of task that they can set and assess tend towards the simplistic, involving tick-boxes and multiple-choice.

In many cases, some or all *support materials* are available on a VLE (for example course handbook, handouts etc.). Announcements can be made, subjects of lectures or seminars publicised and reading lists updated. In some institutions the VLE is the chief medium for communication between tutor and student, so if, for example, a workshop has to be cancelled, that is where the news will be posted.

Supplementary materials might include voluntary exercises, tips to help you tackle writing tasks and links to interesting and relevant sites and materials. There may also be discussion boards or opportunities to post your work for others to view and comment upon.

If your course demands *electronic submission of work*, it will probably be via the VLE.

The value of a VLE depends on its use. A well-thought-out and energetically supported VLE can be an exciting and vibrant addition to your course. On the other hand it can be dispiriting to see one's lonely posted poem languishing without comment in an otherwise deserted site.

Of course, if you're taking a distance learning course, such as those offered by the Open University in the UK, then most of your contact with tutors and fellow students will be 'virtual'.

Seminars and workshops

I didn't know what to expect and I was very naïve to everything, like seminars – was someone going to come and talk at us? I had no idea what to expect at all. (*Student comment*)

Many students confess to being apprehensive about attending their first writing workshop, not least because they don't know what to expect. This section will deal with the main forms and activities of the writing workshop.

The terms 'seminar' and 'workshop' are often used interchangeably. Typically, a workshop is devoted to your own or your fellow students' work, while a seminar might be devoted to writing techniques or themes or exemplary writers. However, examples from other writers are often used as triggers in workshops, and you may be asked to write something based on your discussion of techniques or themes in a seminar.

Physically, the conditions will be similar. You will be in a group of students, with a tutor. Group sizes vary. In the UK, the English Subject Centre, in a recent *Good Practice Guide*, recommended 15, but given financial and timetable pressures you may find yourself in a group of up to thirty. Rooms vary, from 'classroom'-like spaces with ranks of desks through horseshoe or circular configurations to 'boardroom'-style lay-outs (all seated round a table). The Columbia College story method workshop uses a semi-circle of up to 14 people, with no desks, and the tutor in the centre mid-diameter. What will be the case (to start with) is that you will be with a group of strangers and a tutor whom you don't know.

What, then, can you expect in your first workshop? What will your tutor ask you to do?

Get-to-know-you and guidelines

Your tutor will almost certainly instigate an informal 'get-to-know-you' session. These can range from each person simply announcing, in turn, their name, where they're from and what they want from the course, through the 'if you were an ice-cream what flavour would you be?' kind of exercises, to (in extreme cases) primal screaming. Once I was asked to lie on the floor clutching fellow participants in a representation of Rapunzel's hair. You may also be asked to pair off with another student, interview him or her, and then report back to the group.

Having presented a rather jaundiced view of these kinds of events, the plain fact is that you are going to have to get to know these people to some extent. If you're going to get the most out of the course, you're going to have to share your work with them, listen to what they say about it and then act (or not) in the light of that feedback. So this is going to be rather different from, say, an English seminar where, although personal beliefs and values may well come into play, the subject of the discussion is usually the output of an established, absent author.

As well as the get-to-know-you you should expect some guidelines on how to give and receive feedback on work. You will probably be told that comments are about the writing, not the writer; that you shouldn't just say, 'that was good' or 'I liked it', but seek to explain *why* you liked it, what made it work, or not. We will return to this a little later. The pressing question for now is, what kind of work do you actually do in the workshop?

Training and the real event

There are two distinct kinds of workshop activity involving your own and your peers' work:

1   You may be asked to write something in a limited time within the workshop, which you may then be asked to 'share' with the group.
2   You may be invited to bring work in, to be read or acted out and then commented upon. In some cases you may be asked to submit work so that it can be duplicated and distributed before the workshop, so that people have time to look at it carefully and make written comments.

Games and exercises within the workshop

Different tutors have different methods and expectations. Some like participants to get involved on a personal, almost therapeutic, level. We will return to them in a moment. Other tutors (myself included) prefer to make it clear that any exercises you do in class are exactly that – exercises – and not the real thing. Just as a trainer gives an athlete a programme of exercises to prepare for a race, your tutor gives you tasks in preparation for the real thing, namely writing your own work outside of the workshop.

Writing exercises within the workshop are meant to provide artificial inspiration or stimulation. The pattern is usually the same: you are shown/read/made to find something, and then you do some writing based on that something. The 'something' can vary widely: photos, twigs, strange objects, excerpts from exemplary writers and music are all common.

In my view, the key to these exercises is to see them as just that. They are not the 'real thing'. You should not strive to write perfect sentences with perfect structure. The object is to stretch yourself, to find out things you didn't know before and to discover new ways of approaching familiar material. Of course it's difficult if you know the tutor might ask you to read your piece out at the end. You want to impress, you want other people to like what you've written; but if you want to get the most out of the workshop exercise you should try to blank out those considerations and write for yourself, not with the hope of producing a finished piece of work but of mining a nugget or discovering a technique that you can carry away and use in the privacy of your own home (or wherever it is that you work – see Chapter 5).

So, the writing that is produced under the artificial conditions of the workshop isn't important; what is important is understanding the kinds of approaches, techniques and processes to which you as a writer are introduced. It is a common misconception that the inability to produce something wonderful in a workshop session represents failure; far from it. What you are learning are ways to write in the 'real event' later.

However, as I've noted above, some tutors are bolder and more confident. They insist that being 'serious' and treating 'real' issues is important, if not essential, in making workshops worthwhile. They may insist that you 'bring your real self' into workshops. One morning when I asked an unusually anxious-looking student what was the matter, she said that she was taking a Lifewriting module 'and today we're going to start delving'.

Beyond the more harmless games, you may be challenged to 'write down something you don't want anyone else to know about you'. You may be invited to confront something disturbing from your past. You may be asked to write about an unhappy moment. In short, it may be the tutor's aim to bring you to new perspectives and awarenesses through shock and discomfort. In such circumstances you can only go in with an open but questioning mind. Try the exercises and see what happens. You will probably find that you are shaping and censoring what you write with a view to possible 'publication' within the group. Almost certainly you will have some idea of your tutor's expectations, which you will either be trying to satisfy – or possibly disappoint.

Some students find this approach liberating, inspiring, cathartic or mind-expanding; others don't. You should certainly be prepared to give it a go. Remember, as a writer you are trying to learn to see new things and familiar things in a new way. However, when it comes down to it we are all adults: although it may be hard, given a powerful tutor and peer pressure, in the final analysis it is the right of any one of us, when invited to do something, to say, politely, 'no'.

IN PRACTICE

Sample workshop exercises:

1. A 'risky' exercise, by kind permission of poet Tim Liardet (published in the *Guardian*, 13 November 2006):

> In this workshop, I want you to tackle a . . . risky subject which you know will challenge a range of sensitivities, even political correctness. I want you to choose a subject which will be intrinsically difficult to write about, a subject for which you will probably need to test out a range of approaches before you strike the most appropriate one. It can be any subject, as long as it is risky, fraught with pitfalls. Striking the right approach is the preeminent purpose of the exercise . . . Decide on your subject. Don't rush into it. If it makes the hairs stand up on the back of your neck you have probably chosen well. It must have

something to do with taboo. Anything that could prove difficult.

2. A 'safer' exercise courtesy of the author (but which proved terrifying enough for at least one student – see Case Studies):

    A bag of some kind is placed on a central table. It can be any kind of bag, but it may be safest if it is of a kind unlikely to be toted by workshop participants. So, perhaps a dressy handbag, or suitcase, or perhaps a washbag. Then a series of very short exercises:

    (a) Who does it belong to? Can you describe them?
    (b) What's in the bag?
    (c) Put the bag in a place and time. Where are you seeing it? Who's carrying it? Is it the person you first saw?
    (d) Where are they going, and why?
    (e) Look at what you've written. Can you sense a story in the material?

Something you prepared earlier

> The prospect of facing the big wide world is almost as terrifying as having to workshop a piece of creative writing. I thought that it would get easier in the first year, now . . . I've realised it doesn't get any easier and probably never will. (*Third-year student*)

It may be possible to separate yourself from your writing when that writing is done in a few minutes under the artificial conditions of the workshop. It's much harder if you've been invited to submit something you've written in the privacy of your own home to the scrutiny of your peers. A minority of students (like the one quoted above) never get used to this and are still intimidated and lacking in confidence in the final year of the course. Certainly, unless you are extraordinarily confident, or insensitive, when it comes to sharing work for the first time you will be nervous, apprehensive and uncertain how to react to the comments you get. Likewise, when you first hear someone else's work you will probably find it very difficult to respond in a useful way. Most of us hate to offend or upset others.

In an ideal world every workshop group would be made up of mature, sensitive, intelligent and articulate people, all of whom were genuinely committed to improving their own work and that of their peers. But would that be ideal? Would the dynamic of such a group be the best way to move work forward? Such a group wouldn't resemble anything like the audience your work will have to reach if it's going to be published. So perhaps it's a good thing that very rarely will you encounter such an enlightened and supportive environment.

Indeed, it sometimes surprises me that we, as writers, whose main business is the complexity of human interaction, should posit and accept a rather simplistic model for the workshop process and interaction, which largely ignores the people taking part.

What will your group be like? There will of course be a mixture of personalities in your workshop group: the thoughtful, the shy, the garrulous, the assertive, the lazy and, perhaps, the stupid. Where do you fit in? That is a key question to which you need to find an answer.

Meanwhile, someone's work will be read. Usually this is done out loud, though some tutors prefer to let people read the piece silently to themselves. I normally ask someone other than the writer to read work out loud. This allows the writer to concentrate on the words rather than the stress of reading. Also, the way a reader deals with your piece can tell you a lot about which parts work and which don't. If he or she starts to stumble, it's a good clue that there's something amiss with your writing.

After the reading, different tutors adopt different strategies. Some will pitch in themselves straightaway or after a cursory appeal for comments from the group. Others will invite comment from specified individuals. A common model (though impractical with large groups) is known as 'fly-on-the-wall', where the writer is not allowed to comment or respond but must listen as each group member in turn articulates a reaction to the work. The writer then gets a chance to respond, and a general discussion ensues.

This approach prevents the situation where the writer leaps to the defence of his work at the first comment and the discussion turns into an exchange of accusations and denials. It ensures that the writer at least has the opportunity to hear out the comments of his or her peers. Also, of course, it ensures that everyone has the chance (or is forced) to contribute. However, as you wait your turn you may find yourself cursing because someone else has made the point you wanted to make, or desperately casting around for something impressive or interesting to say.

Other tutors at other times may adopt the 'free-for-all' approach where, after the reading, anyone who wants to can pitch in and the writer can respond immediately. Although this has the benefit (in theory) of only having people speak who have something to say, in practice it can happen that no-one says anything, or people with nothing to say say it anyway, and at great length.

To sum up, then, you will have an audience for your work. This is both exciting and frightening. You will be able to gauge how your writing sounds off the page and how people react to it, both initially (in terms of their body language and attention) and then in terms of comments. How do you deal with this feedback?

Dealing with feedback

It's sometimes thought that workshopping is mainly about getting feedback so that you can change a few words here and there in order to 'polish' your piece. This kind of advice may be useful but it is by no means the only or main kind of feedback you'll be looking for. Polishing is a very late and limited form of editing, only appropriate for very nearly finished work (see Chapter 5). It would be an unwise gardener who spent a morning feeding and trimming a tree when he knows he has to chop it down in the afternoon.

To go back to our musical analogy from Chapter 1, polishing is like the learner clarinettist focusing on the precise level of crescendo and diminuendo in a passage, the precise staccato, the imperceptible changes of pace. There's very little point indulging in these niceties if you can't actually play the notes in the right order. Likewise, you as a writer need to get the notes worked out and the overall shape before you attend to details.

Before you workshop a piece you should reflect on why you've written it, what genre it is and what kind of audience you envisage will read it. You might find it helpful to identify areas that you'd like comments on and flag these before the piece is read. For example, does the character of Henry come across as nasty or stupid? Can your peers guess where the story is going? Was the end a surprise? Did they believe that Jane threw herself overboard because of the pizza?

If your peers can be persuaded to jot comments on a hard copy of your writing, all the better. Every reaction is worth considering, even if misguided. Why did that person think Adam was a woman? It takes two to tango, in this case writer and reader, and the mistake may not entirely be due to the stupidity of the latter. Would it be useful to make it even clearer that Adam in your story is a man?

Responses may well vary in terms of the gender of commentators or their age and social background. Your frankly rude poem may delight young men aged 18–22, but may provoke scorn or condescension in older female readers. Is this the reaction you want? Is your audience intentionally limited or would you rather broaden the appeal of your work?

Your tutor will, of necessity, have the most powerful voice in the group. What they say or don't say will carry more weight, whether you agree with it or not. It is worth noting that creative writing isn't an exact science; with the best will in the world it is possible for a tutor to give you useful feedback, for you to act on every point and still not get a perfect final piece of work.

Also it is unusual and probably counter-productive for any teacher to tell you everything that's wrong with your work. Once I demanded that my golf teacher told me everything that was wrong with my swing. Reluctantly he did. After I'd listened for ten minutes to his cogent and detailed analysis of a dozen or so faults I was virtually paralysed and unable to make use of any of his advice. Instead, in a state of mild shock, I laid aside my clubs for a couple of months.

As learners we can only work on a few things at a time. It is the job of a good tutor to identify the most important points for you as a student to work on, before moving on to the next area of weakness.

A good tutor will make sure that what they say is clear, and 'labelled'. You may have made spelling or presentational errors that must be rectified for the piece to be of a professional standard; you may also have made errors of continuity (how did that character get from the shop to the beach?) that should be addressed. But when commenting on matters of style, taste or emphasis, a good tutor should make it clear that you aren't necessarily 'wrong', that these are issues to discuss and think about but not necessarily to change.

It's a great skill to be able to respond to a wide variety of workshop 'advice' in a positive and constructive way. Clearly you can't follow every piece of advice because responses will be contradictory and will range from the astute to the plainly incorrect. A student whom I taught did try to change his work in response to every workshop comment received. The result was disastrous, both for the novel he was writing and for his mental health.

How can you avoid this trap? I suggest you make a note of all reactions, even the wrong ones. Then (a) get an overall feel for the kinds of responses your work is producing; (b) get a more precise sense of the response it's getting from your 'target' audience (if such persons exist within the group); (c) identify aspects that cause confusion.

So, responding in the most fruitful way to workshop feedback is not a simple matter of changing words; it is a complex process that involves evaluating the feedback as honestly and intelligently as you can, being receptive enough to recognise just criticism, yet perceptive and strong enough to reject inappropriate advice. Then you just have the job of finding ways to effectively implement the advice given.

Giving good feedback

You are in the workshop. One of your fellow students has written a poem and brought it in. Perhaps you've had a chance to look at it beforehand. The poem is read out, perhaps by the writer, perhaps by someone else. Now you've got to respond. What should you say?

Although this may seem obvious, it's worth stressing that anything you say should be constructive. You may be tempted to show off your own knowledge or cleverness at the expense of the piece of writing, but this is pointless in the context and can be extremely destructive, not just for the individual concerned but for the group as a whole. If members of a group know that someone will be looking to score points off their work, they will refuse to share their work and the whole process becomes artificial.

Nor should you let your personal likes and dislikes, either of the writer or the writing, emerge in what you say. There is no kind of comment more infuriating than the 'I hate detective fiction' kind. Such a comment is lazy, pointless and irrelevant, unless it prefaces a remark such as 'but I really enjoyed this one', followed by a thoughtful analysis of why they enjoyed it. It is part of the workshop 'contract' that we suspend our personal likes and dislikes and try to help others achieve the best that they can in their chosen form or genre. And, incidentally, it's never a bad idea to try to analyse *why* you don't like a certain genre; I'd even go so far as to recommend that you try writing in it also.

Judge the piece in terms of how far it achieves what the writer wants it to achieve, not what you think it should achieve. For example, if someone wants to write a sci-fi story, it probably isn't helpful for you to tell them that you'd much prefer it if it were a detective piece. If you're not sure what the writer is trying to achieve, ask them questions to clarify. Questions are usually better than statements.

So rather than saying, 'The detective couldn't possibly have known that', it is more helpful to put the question, 'How did the detective find that out?' Or instead of saying, 'I find Henry a really irritating character', you could ask, 'How do you want your readers to react to Henry?'.

A personal rule of mine is to ban comparisons with published/broadcast work. It can be very dispiriting to be told that one's characters are very similar to X and Y in *Eastenders*, or that one's plot is very like that novel by Coetzee. There's nothing new under the sun; there are only seven (some say five or three) stories in the world. They all occur every week in every soap opera. Too acute a sense of the impossibility of true originality can dry you up and stop you from writing. Most writers go through depressing phases where every idea they have immediately reminds them of something else, and so gets trashed.

Our job as writers is to make something new of this shared, familiar material, to make it our own. Constant reference to similar work isn't helpful in my experience. However, by the same token, to allow yourself to go on writing something that is a blatant rip-off (*Willy Winka and the Sherbert Factory*, perhaps), without questioning your position in respect of the plagiarised work is also neither intelligent nor productive (see 'A note on plagiarism' in Chapter 6, p. 98).

IN PRACTICE

Here is an invented workshop piece, with some responses, first (probably) useless, then possibly (but not inevitably) useful:

The airlock hissed open, and Brok vaulted into the antechamber. Two Zxzxian guards blocked his way, but the intrepid aforementioned Brok sprayed them with a hail of incendiary bullets and ran to the far airlock. The airlock hissed open and three Zwzxian guards blocked his way. Brok sprayed them with ionic bio-radiation particles, and they disappeared before his astonished eyes. He dived into the next airlock, and after it had hissed open and he had disposed of the next batch of

Zxzxian guards, he at last stood before the defenceless, bound and gagged princess.

(Probably) useless responses:
1. I don't know why, I just hate science fiction.
2. That's really good it's just like *Star Wars*.
3. Whoever wrote this ought to get out more.
4. I like the word 'vault'.
5. I hate the word 'hissed'.
6. I can see this working really well as a crime novel if you changed all the characters and set it in Swindon.
7. I once wrote a science fiction story, but it was more about the way Einstein's relativity theories impinge on human consciousness – hang on, I think I've got it in my bag somewhere.

Might be useful?
1. I haven't read much science fiction, but I wonder what kind of reader you're writing for?
2. Do you read much science fiction yourself? Which writers do you admire?
3. Where might this kind of story be published?
4. How 'real' do you want your piece to be? How immediate?
5. Is there a reason Brok uses different ammunition in the first two confrontations with the guards, and then no ammunition is specified in the third encounter?
6. Why is Brok 'astonished' by the effect of his radiation weapon?
7. I can really see Brok 'vaulting' out of the airlock the first time, but after that I don't find the writing so immediate and visual.
8. What does Brok think about the princess?
9. What does the princess think about Brok?
10. Does it matter that there is only one female character and she is depicted as a powerless object subject to male domination?

Lapsing into advice:
Did you get bored with writing all those airlock scenes? Maybe you could just have one, and make it longer and more intense? And might it be more effective if the princess at least tried to be more active in the plot – either helping or hindering the rescue?

How much do I have to tell them?

> *I find if I take my best stuff then everyone steals my ideas . . . so I take other pieces in. I work on two different kinds of piece.*

> *If I feel a bit shaky about a poem then I won't bring it in, but if I'm really confident . . .*

> *There's some people I just don't want to show my writing to.*

> *I like to go cos I learn from others but I don't particularly want to read my own.*

The students quoted above have various reasons for not bringing their 'real' (or any) work to workshops.

In this section I want to look at the kind of material you can or should take to the workshop.

When I was interviewed for my first post as a creative writing lecturer the rather uneasy Dean of Humanities asked me what I would do if a student wanted to write pornography. I replied that a writing tutor's job is to facilitate and that, therefore, whatever my own view of a certain genre might be, I should try to help that student make their work as good as it can possibly be in their chosen genre. I didn't get the job.

There is an important point here. How should the tutor and other students react if a student brings disturbing, painful, aggressive or nasty work and wants to share it? On the other hand, what if you write something disturbing or nasty, possibly covering areas about which you know other people in your group may be sensitive?

The usual safety disclaimers are:

- we talk about the writing, not the writer;
- we never assume that the 'I' of a piece is the writer him/herself; and
- we never assume or infer that a piece is autobiographical.

Of course, it's impossible in one's heart to adhere to these guidelines (if your poem is torn to pieces, is it not you who is rent? If Jane writes of self-harm and has fresh razor wounds on her arms, can we ignore them?).

But, whatever one's private surmises or hurts, it is possible and useful to adhere to the guidelines in an operational sense.

Therefore, when your poem is torn to pieces, you *pretend* not to be hurt, and try to extract those constructive parts of the critique and use them to improve the piece. And even if we are convinced that Jane spends most evenings slicing her flesh with a razor, we preserve the convention that the 'Jane' of her poem is a fictional character. Further, if Jane (and this does sometimes happens) *insists* that she is one and the same with the Jane of the poem, that it is 'all true', we still refuse to respond except in terms of the effectiveness of the writing.

Why? Because it's particularly important to learn that having had a Big Experience doesn't necessarily make for an effective piece of writing. As one writer is said to have remarked to a recently bereaved rival, 'That tragic experience was wasted on you'. Or as Margaret Atwood says in *Negotiating with the Dead*:

> A lot of people do have a book in them – that is, they have an experience that other people might want to read about. But this is not the same as 'being a writer' . . . Or, to put it in a more sinister way: everyone can dig a hole in a cemetery, but not everyone is a grave-digger. The latter takes a great deal more stamina and persistence.

So, when a writer, piqued at criticism, complains, 'but it really happened!' we can only answer that that is irrelevant. Just as you should never let the truth spoil a good story, the 'truth' (if such a thing exists) of itself has no merit in writing terms, not least because, as we saw in Chapter 2, the writing makes the reality, and so bad writing will not convey the kind of reality you want to convey.

In my experience groups tend to be self-policing. Unspoken guidelines are established and the occasional rogue piece stands out like a sore thumb. As the weeks progress you will get a feeling for the kind of piece that is 'allowed' and what kind might not be. Of course, this might not be a good thing; it might lead to a split between the work you write for the workshop and what you 'really' write at home. In one sense, if this is the case, it's good to be aware of it. Certainly you shouldn't let your writing be changed simply because you don't feel comfortable sharing it with the workshop group.

Finally, your aim should be to find ways to make workshops as useful for you as they can be. This will involve getting to know your peers and taking their backgrounds and predilections into account when they comment on your work; exactly what any writer has to do in writing for any audience.

Progression

As the course progresses so should you. In the early stages you will be told what to do and will be given fairly well defined tasks. As you progress you should be directing your own study to a much greater extent. For example, most degree courses will ask you in your final year to undertake a dissertation, or dissertation-equivalent project (sometimes termed a 'capstone' module in the US, which often results in a thesis), where assessment goals are negotiated between you and your tutor. You should also be prepared to treat your work more seriously, as 'live' and potentially publishable.

In creative writing progress can be hard to measure. Some students complain that they don't appear to be learning anything or improving. Others claim to detect an imperceptible learning process. If you take the course seriously, then however each assignment turns out, you should be learning and equipping yourself to do better next time.

It's worth stressing that every piece of writing is more than just words on a page. You should treat it like a project, like the building of a bridge: the roadway (text) is the most important manifestation, but there are numerous other considerations involved in planning, shaping and making robust that visible product. Each piece of writing involves problem-solving, which (unless Henry James was right – see Chapter 1) should help in solving the problems of the next piece you write.

Summary

- Most university courses are split up into units or modules. The number of modules you study each year varies from course to course.
- Creative writing is taught by means of a mixture of lectures, tutorials, seminars, workshops and VLEs.
- Workshops are the most widespread form of teaching.
- You may either be asked to bring work you've written earlier to be read out and commented upon, or asked to write something during the workshop, which may also be shared.

Giving and acting on feedback are both difficult skills. Make your own comments useful.

Remeber, any reaction to your own work, however ignorant or inappropriate, is worth considering. How far did your work co-operate in the misunderstanding?

As in any social group, unspoken rules will establish themselves about what kind of writing is acceptable and what isn't. Be aware of these rules, and make sure you aren't censoring yourself unconsciously in order to 'play ball'.

You should expect to get better, not just in terms of finished product but also in terms of your ability to see difficulties and to analyse and deal with them. Every piece of writing is more than words on a page; it's a project, involving numerous other skills and considerations.

5

Assessment

- How will my creative writing be assessed?
- What else will be assessed apart from my creative writing?
- How is assessment checked to make sure it's fair?

Prospective students often ask how their creative writing will be assessed. They are concerned that such judgements depend on personal taste. This chapter will show you the processes involved in the assessment of creative work.

It's subjective, isn't it?

The only thing I was slightly sceptical about was the assessment at the end. I was really curious as to how they'd assess a creative piece of work.

You know, what someone else finds interesting or good, someone else thinks is crap.

It's subjective, isn't it, with a story?

I don't know how they judge it cos it's always going to be slightly –
well quite a lot – subjective.

(Student comments about assessment)

Are these students right? Is assessment subjective? Does the grade you get
depend not on the intrinsic qualities of your work but on the personal
likes and dislikes of your marker? Before moving to assessment in your
course it will be useful to look at the assessment of writing in the 'real'
world.

Assessment in the writing industries

Writers outside educational settings are assessed all the time. The work of
novelists, for example, is assessed by agents and editors; most publishers
have a, sometimes huge, 'slush pile' of unsolicited manuscripts. Do they
find it difficult to judge these submissions? The short answer is 'no'; most
of the submissions will simply not be of a publishable standard and can
be safely returned with a standard rejection slip.

This assessment has nothing to do with personal taste, it has to do
with quality of the writing and presentation. However, once the editor
is left with those manuscripts that are potentially of a publishable
standard, do they accept or reject simply on the basis of personal taste at
this stage?

The answer is again, no. The next question after general quality is
particular fitness for purpose. If you send an article about fly fishing to a
knitting magazine, or a television script to a publisher of novels, it doesn't
matter how good your writing is, they won't buy it. The same goes for
kinds of novel, kinds of script and kinds of poetry. Editors themselves
know the kind of list they publish. It is also common practice now
for sales and marketing people to be involved at the commissioning stage
for works of fiction. They have to be persuaded that a book will appeal to
booksellers and to a public. So if I'm an editor in a publishing house,
however much I love a particular book, I will have to convince a lot of
other people of its merit and marketability before it will be commis-
sioned. Then, after books are published, they are assessed by bookstore
reps, bookstore staff, purchasers and reviewers, before they finally
become subject to the personal taste of readers.

A television scriptwriter working for a drama series or soap opera will
have even more scrutiny and assessment at the beginning of this process,

in the form of story editors, script editors, continuity editors, producers, executive producers and the like. What the scriptwriter writes must fit in with the overall tone of the series and must take stories along in the desired direction and at the pace required, without contradicting events in the past or in the projected future.

So, if I'm a script editor for a popular soap opera, I might love a particularly poetic script, but I can't use it in that form because it won't fit the brief and tone of the programme; nor can I go along with a writer who kills off a character who is already written into subsequent episodes or (as this writer once did) uses a location that is not provided for in the studio.

The plain fact is that the whole writing industry is based on assessment, and this assessment is complex, involving both the intrinsic qualities of the work and the demands of the specific market or slot. Some element of subjectivity may be involved in the selection of writers, but this cannot be the controlling principle in the selection of books, poems and scripts.

The question remains, how much of this 'real world' assessment is present, or appropriate, in the university setting?

Assessment criteria

As a student at a university or college you should be shielded both from excessive subjectivity on the part of your markers and excessive reference to the 'marketability' of your writing. Institutions achieve this by setting out clear assessment criteria, and you should be given a copy of the criteria relevant to your course.

In the UK these criteria are normally set out in great detail (too much detail, some might say) at different levels within the institution. So, for example, there will almost certainly be

- *general criteria* set at institutional level;
- *subject criteria* set at subject level; and
- *module/unit criteria* set at the level of the particular unit or module you are taking.

If your subject is part of a faculty, or school, then there may also be criteria set at that level also, though for the sake of clarity I won't consider that level here.

It's impossible to generalise about criteria, so you need to find out those that apply for the course you are taking. However, it may be useful for you to see a concrete example so that you can begin to understand the kind of measures that might be in place to make your assessment as fair and transparent as possible.

Let's look, then, at the criteria given for achieving a distinction (a mark of 70 per cent or more) at my own institution. The *institutional* guidelines read as follows:

> Work of distinguished quality, which is based on extensive research and/or strong technical and creative competence. Clear and logical organisation; consistent scheme of references, used entirely appropriately. An authoritative grasp of concepts, methodology and content appropriate to the subject/discipline and to the assessment task ... There is clear evidence of originality and insight and an ability to sustain an argument and/or solve discipline-related problems, based on critical analysis and/or evaluation. The ability to synthesise material effectively and the potential for skilled innovation in thinking and practice will be evident.

These criteria apply not just to creative writing but to Geography, Dance, Business Studies, Remote Sensing and all the other subjects taught at the institution. Are these criteria relevant to creative writing? Surely the answer must be 'yes'. 'Creative competence', 'originality', 'the ability to sustain an argument and/or solve discipline-related problems', 'the ability to synthesise material' and 'skilled innovation in thinking and practice' are all qualities relevant to – maybe essential for – effective creative writing; and other qualities listed (for example 'extensive research' and 'a consistent scheme of references, used entirely appropriately') relate to the *contextualising* or *reflective* aspect of the writing course (see 'Non-creative assessment items', p. 76).

Nor should we forget 'clear and logical organisation'; though some late romantics might favour what Lawrence Ferlinghetti, in his poem 'Autobiography', terms 'wild stories without punctuation', it seems to me no bad thing to learn how to present your material in a way that is accessible to your reader.

At *subject* level we find:

Creative work achieving this grade will show an impressively full control of language and structure – technical control, control of literary form and control of voice, style, idiom and register. The work will be striking and original; phrases, lines, characters, descriptions, moments, dramatic events or explorations of fictional settings may be eloquent and memorable. The subject-matter of the work will have been explored intelligently, with insight and breadth of viewpoint. An impressive knowledge and understanding of both form and subject-matter will be evident. Creative writing in this category will show a clear understanding of the reader's needs and those of genre: it may show vividness and originality within the rules and conventions of genre or it may challenge or break those rules and conventions in a vivid and effective way, for carefully considered reasons (which will be explained in the critical commentary).

This paragraph serves to particularise the general qualities outlined in the institutional guidelines. The emphasis is on *control* and *knowledge*. You will be expected to know what you are writing, and who you are writing it for. You will be expected to have read widely in the kind of genre you are attempting. Your own work should be informed by this knowledge and should show control of the particular traits and techniques of that genre. If you depart from the 'rules and conventions', you must demonstrate that you know what those rules and conventions are and have good reason for breaking with them.

At *module* or *unit* level, those 'rules and conventions' are spelt out, and the techniques relevant to the particular activity or literary form are identified. Here's an example, taken from a level one module at Bath Spa University:

**CS1006: Writing, the Process – CASE STUDY –
ASSESSMENT CRITERIA**
Deadline – Friday 17th December 2004
1250 words maximum – 40% of total mark

- **You will be asked to write a case study based on the origin and growth of a piece or pieces of your own work.**

Assessment of your case study will be based on:

- Your ability to analyse when and why you started taking the idea seriously.
- Your ability to identify for which genre or market it is suitable.
- Your ability to establish the scale or scope of the piece of work.
- Or, if you abandoned it, your ability to note when and why you decided to do so.
- Your ability to describe the style and tone of your piece.
- Your ability to set your case study in the context of the writing (prose, poetry or script) or media (i.e. film, TV, music, commercials, etc.) that have influenced you and describe how these influences helped to shape your idea.
- Your ability to describe your intentions in writing your piece and what you hoped to achieve.
- Your ability to express your ideas clearly without grammatical or spelling errors.

More generally, your work should also evidence the following learning outcomes, as per the module syllabus:

2. a developing understanding of your own habits and beliefs in relation to creative composition.
4. a basic understanding of the different kinds and levels of editing required at different stages of the creative process.
5. the ability to organise your time to support your writing.
6. the ability to reflect critically on your work in preparation for editing and redrafting.
7. the ability to apply different levels of editing skills to your own and other people's work.

Of course, it's not enough just to do these things; you must do them well in order to score well.

In the US, although assessment criteria may not be so exhaustive, they are seen to be of growing importance by education authorities. This Columbia College statement of criteria for a Fiction Writing course perhaps stresses *improvement, process* and *participation* rather more than the UK example, but the parallels are still clear:

Grades are determined holistically, taking into account the following criteria:

A. Attendance: No more than three absences. Not negotiable.
B. Page counts: 60 pages of writing exhibiting reasonable effort and responding to class assignments. Not negotiable.
C. Assignments: Completion of all reading and writing assignments fully and on time – counts heavily.
D. Progress: Overall quality and improvement – counts heavily.
E. Full movements: Good examples of assignments, rewritten where necessary, and two full movements (short stories or chapters), at least one of which has been rewritten to bring it as close as possible to publishable quality.
F. Class participation: Good effort and full engagement in class activities.
G. Promptness: Getting to class on time at beginning and after break.
H. Manuscripts: All work must be proofread, professional in appearance.
I. Students caught plagiarizing work will receive the grade of F. Not negotiable.

One point is worth stressing: generally, you can't just write well to score well. To take an extreme and particular example, if you are taking a unit called 'Writing Science Fiction' and you submit work that (whatever its intrinsic quality) has no elements of science or fiction in it, then you cannot expect to get a good grade. However, where assessment in a creative writing course context differs most significantly from 'real world' assessment is that in the former there will normally be part of the assessment where you are able to explain what you were trying to do, what target you have set yourself, and why. To this element of assessment we will turn now.

Non-creative assessment items

It is normal practice in creative writing courses that, apart from producing a piece or pieces of writing for assessment, you will also have to write an accompanying critical, reflective or contextualising piece. Recent research conducted by Robert Sheppard and Scott Thurston for the English Subject Centre in the UK reveals a wide variety of names and forms for these non-creative elements, including reflection, self-assessment, critique, commentary, journal, poetics, critical commentary, self-reflective essay and critical preface. Non-creative assessments such as these are becoming more and more common in the US, partly because they provide validation and partly because they help students to accelerate their ability to understand and monitor their own writing processes.

We have already touched on the educational justification for these elements in Chapter 2. In order to have credibility as a degree programme a university creative writing course must do more than 'just' teach you to write well. It is primarily in the non-creative assessment items that you can demonstrate what you have learned outside of the finished writing product.

The most common kinds of non-creative assessments are:

1. Self criticism/assessment/reflection: You discuss your aims in writing your piece, its genre and what influenced your writing, and you assess its strengths and weaknesses.

2. A critical essay: You write a critical piece discussing published writing in the area you are studying (for example, if you are studying writing for television, you might write about three television dramatists).

3. The technical essay: You are asked to write about technical features such as humour or suspense, not necessarily limited by genre.

Often a single assessment item will ask you to combine two or all three of these approaches.

As part of the non-creative assessment you may also be invited (or compelled) to keep some kind of notebook or journal in which you record what you read, what you think of what you read, ideas, notes from workshops and lectures etc. Here, for example, are the suggested and progressive weekly journal assignments for the Fiction Writing II course (Parody) at Columbia College, Chicago:

1. Responses to the assigned readings.
2. Structural lists drawn from the published models.
3. Discussion of students' material, patterns in things chosen to be written and read, current concerns (social, political, etc.) that might play a part in their parody material.
4. Discussion of the use of point-of-view.
5. Discussion of the process of writing the parody, problems and solutions, discoveries made, etc.
6. Continued response to published work, emphasis on things discovered on second and third readings.
7. Further discussion on structure as applied to student's work other than parody.
8. Discussion on style as it pertains to a variety of published reading and student's own work.

Common to all these items is *reflection* on your own work and the work of others, and the *contextualisation* of your writing. Again, the untaught, intuitive genius, who simply writes what inspiration dictates and leaves it to posterity to be his or her judge, may feel at a disadvantage here. However, the counter-arguments are, first, that you won't know what you've learned, or be able to consolidate it, until you reflect on what you've done; and secondly, a university creative writing course isn't usually just a writing course – there are other places to go 'just' to learn to write.

So what kinds of contextualisation are relevant for you? One key assessment criterion is likely to be how far you as a writer have understood a particular form or genre, and have shaped your writing with this knowledge in mind. You will therefore have to carry out some research. For example, if you are writing science fiction, you should be able to demonstrate that you know what science fiction is (or if there is no clear definition, show that you are aware of the debate and issues surrounding that lack of definition). You should also have some knowledge of the *history* of the genre and *current publishing practice and opportunities*. This will involve both the reading of books and stories, looking at who publishes them, where and in what form.

This background knowledge will then enable you to place your own work in the overall context of the genre both historically and as it stands now, and will also allow you to indicate clearly and intelligently why you have broken rules, if that's what you have chosen to do. It is an old truism that you must know what the rules are before you can break them.

To go back to our earlier hypothetical example of a piece of writing submitted for a science fiction course that appears to have no science and no fiction in it: if you can intelligently and persuasively explain in the commentary why this is the case, you may still be able to score well.

And this brings us to one of the great (and often unsung) advantages of the non-creative piece; it does give you the chance to show off the work you've done and what you've learned, even if your creative work happens, for whatever reason, not to be of the highest quality. This is a luxury not granted to a writer outside the academy, where bad work means instant and irredeemable rejection.

The extent to which the non-creative assessment element can 'rescue' the flawed creative work of course depends on the way the marks are weighted, and there is wide variation both across the sector and within individual institutions and modules. You may find separate grades are given for the two elements, in which case the weighting of marks can vary from 50/50 to 80/20 (in either direction). In some cases, a 'global' mark is awarded, where creative and non-creative elements are taken as a whole. This can favour either the untaught genius whose reflection is severely limited, or the perpetrator of a 'glorious failure' in creative terms, which generates a superb piece of reflection, commentary and analysis.

One final point: creative writing students can be negative and dismissive about non-creative assessment elements. I would only point out that professional writers have to deal with a wide variety of non-creative pieces of writing: letters to agents and editors, synopses and treatments of their work, CVs, blurbs and pitches. And, if anything, these pieces of writing need to be even more thoroughly edited and targeted than the creative work itself. Just because a piece of writing is non-creative is no excuse for treating it in a slapdash way. On the contrary, there's even more reason for making it informative and entertaining.

IN PRACTICE

Here are the guidelines I prepared for the 'non-creative' assessment item for a Level 2 Scriptwriting module. You could try applying them to something you've written yourself.

THE COMMENTARY: there's plenty to say.

Guidelines: Don't follow these points slavishly. Use those things that are or were important to your writing.

A. Plays you've read, heard or watched: techniques/effects you imitated, or liked; techniques/effects that didn't work. Other books, critical, theoretical, which have influenced your approach.

B. Characters: How did your characters develop? From 'real' people? Were they demanded by the plot? How did you find their voices? Did the dreaded soap effect happen with any of them?

C. Story: Where did the idea come from? Newspapers, other plays, books, your own experience? How did it develop? Did it have a suitable climax or did you have to change the original idea to make an effective play?

D. Structure: How did you go about structuring the play? How did you decide where to start, where to finish and what scenes were necessary or effective? What scenes did you try out and discard?

E. Writing process: Did you start with sketches, experiments or monologue? If so, why not give brief examples, and talk about them? Did you start at the beginning and try and work through? If so, did you get stuck at some points? If so, analyse why you got stuck.

F. Writing habits: When did you write? Did you have set times? Were you often interrupted? Were there particular circumstances where you wrote well? Did you use notebooks? If so, what kind? Big official-looking ones, or scraps of paper? Did you sometimes fail to write down ideas when they came to you, and then forget what they were? Did you find it hard to discipline yourself? Did you look forward with joy to writing your play? If not, why not? NOTE: ANYONE USING THE WORD 'INSPIRED' WITHOUT RIGOROUSLY DISCUSSING A DEFINITION OF THE SAME IN RELATION TO SELF WILL BE SEVERELY PENALISED.

G. The course: Were there things we did in the workshops that helped you? Likewise hindered? How did you find the group work aspect? Being asked to read or perform? Did the writing you did in workshop exercises influence your real writing outside of the classroom?

H. Your play: What kind of play is it? Is it large-scale, popular or small-scale fringe theatre? Who will want to see it? Is it TV? If so, what slot, what channel? Film: you might like to suggest some actors. If part of a larger whole, give a brief synopsis (as far as you can) of the rest of the piece, with an idea of total length and where your submission fits in.

I. Appendices: If you've done loads of work/revision, then flaunt it. Don't be afraid to submit (brief) examples of drafts or other plays or fragments as appendices, with brief discussion of same in the commentary.

J. This section is intentionally blank.

K. To those who say 1500 words is not enough, I point to the haiku writer who yearns for extra syllables. The commentary, like the haiku, is a form, and it's up to you to get the most out of it. This in itself is a test. Writing with the word count on and stopping when you hit the limit probably won't allow you to exploit the form to the full.

FINALLY:

Try to write clearly.
Don't feel you have to adopt a strange strained pseudo-'official' academic tone.
Treat the commentary as an exploration: it may not end up with neat, straightforward answers.
Treat the commentary with respect: it is an important part of your assessment, and will probably take much thought and much revision.

ALWAYS QUESTION THE TERMS YOU USE. ASK ONE QUESTION MORE. IF YOU WRITE: 'I don't know where my play came from, I just wrote it', fair enough, I respect your position, but you will get an extremely low grade.

OH, AND ANOTHER THING: contrary to popular belief, the commentary is meant to be of benefit to YOU. Bear that in mind when deciding how to approach it.

Other assessment methods

Some courses also use performances or presentations (some of which include peer assessment), and examinations or timed exercises. So, if you're taking a course in performance poetry it seems only fair to expect you to perform. You might be observed by more than one marker, and be recorded, either on camera or by sound alone, especially if your institution uses an external examiner. Assessment criteria should make clear the balance between content and performance in the assessment.

Presentations are often given in groups, rather than individually. You might have to work in a team on a contextualising theme, or making a film, or putting together a performance, for example. Often in these team assessments a group mark is given, though this can sometimes be varied according to the examiners' assessment of each individual's contribution. Even so, it's clear that in group work, if anyone doesn't pull their weight the whole will suffer.

You may be invited to grade your peers' work after these sessions, with the possibility that the examiners take your marks into account when deciding their own. This is **peer assessment**.

Examinations are rare in creative writing, though not unknown. Examination questions could involve writing about other writers, or about writing techniques, or could involve practical writing tasks. For example, you might be given material that you are required to transform in some way: say a passage of tragic prose that you must rewrite in a different tone or from a different point of view.

Timed exercises demand similar activities, but instead of going to an examination room you are given the material and have to hand your response in within, say, a week.

Assessments will normally have a word limit, or word guideline. This will vary with genre and topic. For more on word counts, and how to approach them, see Chapter 6.

Assessment, feedback and monitoring

When you get your assessed work back, you should also expect feedback from your marker explaining your mark. It is tempting just to look at the marks or grades you're given and not pay attention to your tutor's comments. You might argue that you've been getting feedback all the way through your course, if you were regularly workshopping your writing. This informal feedback is important and you should consider it carefully, but it's worth bearing in mind that assessment is a time when you can expect just that: not just helpful and encouraging advice but also a realistic calibration of the standard of your writing, and hence a chance to gauge your progress.

Speaking personally, as a marker I will approach your work in a quite different way than when I am teaching. When teaching I will concentrate on what you do well and on a few points that I consider important, which I think you can readily act upon. When I'm marking I will of course praise those things that seem good in your work, but I will also try to give at least an indication of all the areas that need improvement.

Remember, although the units of study you take may be single and isolated, you as a person and a writer are not segmented, and advice given at the end of, say, an Intermediate Poetry unit may well be useful as you move on to an advanced course, or, for that matter, in a subsequent prose unit. So if you don't understand or agree with your tutor's feedback, why not make an appointment to see them and discuss it?

It is worth pointing out that, in a university or college setting, assessment should be monitored. Monitoring methods might include second marking within the institution, the use of an external examiner and examination boards where an overview of assessment is possible.

Attendance

Here are some students' answers to the question, 'Can you get a good grade without attending classes?':

I think it's wonderful. I'm one of those who can do that. I've passed all my modules. Every subject I've ever done I've done the night before, and got pretty damn good marks.

That really bugs me.

What's the point of doing it if you're not going to attend?

If you do well *without* lectures, how much better are you going to do by going?

Treatment of attendance varies widely from institution to institution. In some, both in the UK and US, if you miss a certain number of sessions without good reason you are removed from the course. Attendance is good at those institutions, though registers must be kept very carefully so as to leave no room for doubt or error about someone's presence or absence.

At the other extreme, some institutions, while officially stating that 'attendance is mandatory', don't actually do anything if you don't turn up, apart from perhaps sending you a letter. Between these extremes are various regulations including a sliding scale of marks deducted, depending on the number of sessions missed, or the taking of attendance into account when deciding whether to allow students who fail to retake the unit.

Your tutors will want you to attend for a variety of reasons:

- They feel they are offering you the benefit of their knowledge, and if you don't attend you are slighting them.
- If you don't attend, you won't have done any assignments or preparation for the following session, and so won't be in a position to take part effectively.
- It is very irritating to have to explain again and again what was done the previous week for the benefit of non-attenders.
- Creative writing workshops depend to a large extent on developing trust among the group. Non-attenders will find it hard to participate in this network of trust.
- Overall it makes it very hard for your tutor to put together a coherent and progressive course if he or she can't be sure from week to week who's going to be there and what bits they've missed.

Of course, there are many reasons for non-attendance. You may be genuinely sick, or have personal problems. You may well have to work, in order to support yourself, and your boss demands that you work when you'd rather be in a workshop. You may have transport problems, or you may feel that given the assessment items (let's say a story and a commentary), you're quite capable of doing them in your own time without all the bother of going to workshops and meeting up with other people week after week.

If you don't attend you will certainly miss out on the (often unassessed) benefits of doing creative writing: collaboration, participation, learning how to give and take constructive criticism, learning how to work with other people in project management – and a lot of fun. You may also find that you have missed crucial specific guidance about how you should approach an assessment item, which could result in your getting a very poor score.

And while all tutors are (I'm sure) scrupulously professional about their marking, it might not be a surprise if, in borderline cases, they were inclined to give the benefit of the doubt to a conscientious student and not to someone who has spurned the tutor's pearls of wisdom all term.

Final word

I'll leave the final word on assessment (perhaps, on the face of it, rather a cruel one) to a student:

> At first there was a collective sense of indignation at the thought of work being graded: 'How can they possibly mark creative work?' 'It's a matter of taste, surely?' However, as soon as you heard something truly, truly dreadful or something truly, truly wonderful, a kind of polarisation occurred. I believe that in our first big workshops we could tell very quickly just how possible it is to grade creative work. It doesn't take much to separate the shit from the sugar.

Summary

- Some people think that it's impossible to grade creative writing, that it all depends on personal taste.
- Creative writing in the 'real' world is assessed all the time by a wide variety of interested parties, based on a wide variety of criteria.
- In an academic context there are also criteria that govern assessment.
- To an extent, how you will be assessed depends on what you have attempted to achieve, and there is often an opportunity in a non-creative assessment item or items to spell this out to your assessor.
- Your attendance at teaching sessions might influence the marks you get, either directly or indirectly.

PART III

WRITERS' HABITS, WRITERS' SKILLS

6

Developing your own working habits

- How much time should I spend working?
- What can I do if I'm not inspired?
- Why should I read books?
- What books should I read?

This chapter looks at the different kinds of work involved in doing creative writing. In particular we will look at the ways in which you can organise yourself and your time outside of the workshop to best effect. It is important to realise that creative writing is perhaps one of the hardest subjects in terms of motivation and self-direction.

Tough to do at home

What we were doing today, that's quite a hard thing to do at home. (Comment by a student after a workshop)

What does this student mean? To explain, we need to look at your time commitment on the course. Most courses prescribe an indicative total of hours that a student should expect to work. This includes a *contact* quota and also a *self-directed* element. Although contact time varies (for example, in the US you might have up to 20 hours in the classroom, as opposed to half or less than that in the UK), the rest of your working week (say 20–30 hours if you are a full-time student) you are expected to organise yourself.

This will be the same whatever subject you're studying, but there is an element of self-direction from the early stages of a creative writing course that you don't find in many others. While with other subjects tasks may appear to be more or less well defined (an essay on *Romeo and Juliet*, say, with title provided), in creative writing much of the time you will be defining 'the job' yourself (a story – about what? what style? for what kind of audience?). This is much harder, but also much more rewarding if you get it done.

This chapter aims to help you to understand how to use your time when doing creative writing, and to get the writing job done.

Where to write

You've just had a writing workshop. It's been a very positive experience. You've done several exercises, shared some of the results with your fellow students who've been supportive and encouraging, your tutor has been inspirational and you're buzzing with energy. What do you do now? You can't just wait till next week. More than half of the work you're expected to do is on your own. So the first question to answer is 'Where you are going to work'.

If you think that where writers work is a trivial or irrelevant matter for enquiry I can point you to the fact that the British Society of Authors, in 2005, launched an appeal to members to send photographs of their workspace in order to build up an archive for future research and posterity. Why? Because where we work *does* have an immense bearing on how and what we write.

One obvious place to do all or some of this work is in your home. What will your 'home' be while you're doing creative writing?

Many students now remain in their family home. If this is the case for you, you will be surrounded by people who are probably supportive but who may also have expectations based on the 'old' you, and may find it hard to understand what you are doing for your studies. This can be even more difficult for mature students with children, who see a parent at home as 'available'.

This issue can be made harder if the subject you're doing is creative writing. This is a dialogue reported by one student:

Parent: What are you doing?
Student: Working.
Parent: What work is that?
Student: I'm writing a story.
Parent: Oh, I thought you meant real work.

The same undermining dialogue can occur if you happen to be living away from home, perhaps in shared accommodation, especially if your flatmates are doing more conventional degrees. Sitting alone in your bedroom with sceptical people just outside your door can add up to loss of motivation and confidence.

The first thing to say is that most published writers report similar difficulty in establishing a credible sense of self as writer and a dynamic pattern of working. When I first tried to write professionally I used to go to the library to work. Why? Because it seemed more 'official' – more like a real job, real work (though I still covered my manuscript with my forearm if someone passed behind me).

There's no hard-and-fast rule about where to work. Novelist Caryl Phillips likes to stay in hotels to work. Some writers can work in public places (J. K. Rowling in a café, Maureen Duffy in coffee bar or pub), others require seclusion in a private place (Roald Dahl and others in their sheds).

Stephen King, in *On Writing*, stresses the importance of having a door that you are able and willing to close. Perhaps this is the key point for you as a creative writing student, whether you are sitting in a café or locked in your shed: the ability to focus on your own work and to take yourself seriously. Wherever you decide to write, you must treat your writing as work just like work in any other subject.

When to write

In Chapter 1 we explored the idea that in order to get better at writing you need to practise. In order to practise you need time. Therefore it seems logical to set aside certain times during the week for writing, just as if you were learning the clarinet you might set aside certain time for practice.

There are some writers (like novelist John Harvey) who stick to a routine, sometimes to the extent of treating writing as a 9 to 5 job. Others fit writing in on top of a career. For example, Anthony Trollope,

Victorian author of the *Barsetshire Chronicles*, who would rise at 5 a.m., write 1000 words, and then go to his day job with the Post Office (where, incidentally, he invented the pillar-box).

Most of us work better at certain times of the day (or night). Again, there's no hard-and-fast rule. My own impression, gathered from writers talking and writing about the writing process, is that perhaps the most common model is (as is the case with novelist Mark Illis) 'actual' writing in the morning, and other tasks (such as research, networking, editing, planning, income tax) in the afternoon and evening.

The important thing is to try to find out when you work best, and then set aside blocks of time for your writing. This may be difficult, especially if you're studying subjects other than writing at the same time, which may have very real and unavoidable tasks and deadlines. It is not uncommon for students who are doing Creative Writing in combination with another subject to say things like, 'I didn't have time to do any writing this week because I had too much work set for Textiles' (or whatever).

Yes, if you have to prioritise assignments, it's perhaps easier to explain away why you didn't do a writing assignment (you weren't inspired) than, say, an English essay. And let's be honest, when it comes to prioritising work, it is not only tempting but practical and professional to look ahead to assessments, both their content and timing. Why am I working on this book now, and not one of the other assignments I've got? Because the deadline for this one is only two weeks away.

So, if you are doing creative writing in combination with, say, English, and you look ahead to the assessment items, and see that for English you have to write a 1500-word essay about *Moll Flanders*, while for creative writing you have to write a 1500-word story, which one are you tempted to prioritise? The work involved in the *Moll Flanders* assignment before you can write the essay is pretty obvious. For a start, you must read the book and make notes, and probably read some critical works too. You then have to organise what you've done in such a way that you can answer the essay question. So, it may well seem that these tasks are much more pressing than to start work on a story that is only 1500 words long, and not due in for another three months. It is my task in this section to disabuse you of this notion.

Word counts: the false gods

There's an old saying that 'every book starts with a single word'. What the saying fails to make clear is that that single word is almost certainly not the first word that the writer wrote. This can seem puzzling for someone new to the process. As readers we are used to books (or stories or plays) as a linear journey, from start to finish. As literary critics, although we may move around the work, tracing themes and comparing characters, we still think of it as a completed thing with a set order. It is natural to assume that the writer conceived it and wrote it in that order, starting on page one and working through to the end.

This is almost certainly not the case, but it is a misconception on which many beginners base their action plan regarding assignments. In short, you may be tempted to see word counts as a 'finishing line' to sprint towards, stagger across and stop. You may be tempted to think, 'Well, if that's all we've got to do, it surely won't take much work. I can start it a week or so before the hand-in date and get it done-and-dusted no trouble'. You may even tell yourself that you can only work to deadlines, that you find it impossible to do any work until under that kind of pressure.

Maybe; but it's only fair to say that this approach will not benefit you as a student or a writer, and will almost certainly not achieve the best grades. One of the most common reasons for any writer to get stuck with a piece of writing is the misconception that the first sentence they write will be the first sentence of the finished piece. And I can attest, even at my advanced stage of life, to having made the same mistake with my last book. I wrote a page of purple prose to open it, which I loved and wouldn't change. I clung on to it for three years, during which every attempt to get the book to work stalled. At last I took advice from my editor, cut the purple page, and the book suddenly made sense.

So if you're not going to start at the beginning and work through to the end, how does good writing get written? An analogy might be a bridge. To look at, its construction is straightforward; it starts on this side of the river and, supported by a succession of pillars, stretches to the far side. We cross it in linear fashion. Surely then that's the way it was built? Hardly. You wouldn't get very far beyond the first span using such a method. And, writing a book, you probably won't get far beyond page 5 working in linear fashion. The bridge is built to a plan. The builder knows where it's going. It then proceeds by a series of stages that are not linear: explorations, soundings, drillings, foundations (now invisible), then pillars, supports, crossbracings, and finally roadway. It's the roadway that we see, and use, and the roadway is like the text of the book we read; it is the final result of a complex process.

Just as the essay on *Moll Flanders* demands a lot of work outside the actual writing, so will any good piece of creative writing. What kind of work I'm talking about we will discuss in the next section.

Writing isn't just writing

It's obvious what you have to do before you can write your *Moll Flanders* essay – read the book for a start. The work required before you can produce a good piece of writing is less obvious, and less clearly structured. Different writers will approach the task in different ways and with their own emphasis on the various strategies. That's why doing creative writing requires more self-discipline than many other subjects: no-one can offer you a methodology 'off the peg' that is guaranteed to work for you.

Here I will offer you a broad outline of ways in which you can approach a project before or in parallel with the 'real' writing. I stress that these approaches are neither exhaustive nor mandatory; they are a synthesis of approaches that I have found useful, or which have been recommended by other writers and teachers. I only suggest you bear them in mind when thinking of starting a piece of writing. You can:

- *experiment*;
- *analyse*; and
- *research*.

Experiment involves writing, but the trick is that you're not committing yourself to the awful and irrevocable 'Chapter 1, Page 1'.

One of the best-known images of the writer (and least useful for someone learning to write) is the hyper-self-critic who types a sentence, immediately re-reads it and then rips the sheet out of the typewriter, screws it up and tosses it into the wastebin. Of course, we don't tend to use typewriters these days, but the underlying principle is still very common. It's very easy to write something, look at it, wince and discard it, and perhaps tell yourself that you're not inspired today or even that you've got writer's block.

If you were learning to play the clarinet, you wouldn't expect to play a piece perfectly first time. You'd expect to play wrong notes, run through it slowly, isolate the difficult bits, and gradually work it up to speed. Why should it be different with writing? You have to get things wrong before you can get them right.

That's where experiment comes in. Let's say you have an idea for a story about a girl with a parrot whom she loves but also neglects. Experiments could involve any or all of the following (or something completely different):

- Try to think yourself inside the girl's head. Let her talk about the parrot outside of the story. What does she think of him? What does he mean to her? Does she start talking about other things? Her mother, her father, her boyfriend?
- Do the same from the parrot's point of view.
- Write a passage, where something crucial or exciting happens between them, in the third person.
- Write it again in the first person.
- Ask some practical questions like, who bought the parrot, and why? Who cleans it out? Where is its cage in the house?
- Try some opening sentences.
- Try some closing sentences.

What you are doing is feeling out your material, getting to know your characters and getting a sense of what the piece is about and where it wants to go. You're not trying to write great literature, or perfect sentences; you're rather like a painter sketching in charcoal before applying paint, like an athlete doing exercises in training for the main event, the race (real writing). And if by chance some of the stuff you write happens to be suitable for inclusion in the final piece, all well and good – but don't bank on it. In experimental work you must give yourself licence to 'fail' in terms of polished, finished product.

Analysis goes hand in hand with experiment, but uses your *rational* rather than your *intuitive* faculties. So while you're experimenting, you should also be asking yourself questions about the results of the experimentation:

- Whose story is it (girl, parrot or someone else entirely)?
- What is the hero/ine seeking?

- What's stopping them getting it?
- Do they get it in the end?
- Is it a happy ending?
- Where are you going to start?
- Why now? What kicks the story started at this particular moment?

You may also like to write character breakdowns for your characters (e.g. age, gender, likes, dislikes, hair colour, etc.), draw maps of towns and plans of houses – but now we're moving towards research.

Research will be indicated where experiment and analysis reveal that you don't know something it would be very useful to know. For our parrot story research might include:

- Visiting a parrot shop to see how they behave;
- Getting books or magazines about parrots and their country of origin;
- Browsing the internet for similar;
- Going somewhere where the story is set; and
- Reading other books (this topic deserves a section to itself).

Reading as a writer

There are a huge variety of ways of reading as a critic, and here is not the place to explore them. Suffice to say that critical approaches tend to be based on writing as *finished product*, and on what it *means*. As writers, we are concerned with *how it was made* and *how it works*.

If you are studying, say, creative prose writing, there is no standard 'canon' as you will find in English literature. Different tutors will use different examples to help you develop your own skills and style. Again, this lack of definition can be disturbing or bewildering to someone new to creative writing.

One of my students recently responded to the task of writing an analysis of two other writers' working methods and comparing them to his own, with an exasperated: 'Which writers? When?' The answer is, of course, any writers, the writers that you have found in your research to be most relevant and useful. Again, it is an example of how doing creative writing demands more self-direction than other programmes.

Why are you expected to read? For a start, if you're interested in writing it would seem logical that you take an interest in the writing of others (although not every student of writing sees it this way). As Dr Johnson is reputed to have said:

> The greatest part of a writer's time is spent in reading, in order to write: a man will turn over half a library to make one book.

The library is a vast storehouse of captive 'inspiration' waiting to be unleashed on our imagination. There are numerous ways that other books can feed into your work. For example:

1 Exemplary books on a similar topic.
2 'Factual' books to give background.
3 Books with a special kind of voice that suits your subject matter (imitation).
4 Books as market research.

Exemplary books on a similar topic

When I wrote my first novel for the teenage female market, I read a lot of books written for that market. Why? Because I didn't know the conventions, I didn't know what the readers were used to, I didn't know how much foul and abusive language was permitted and I didn't know what the characters were allowed to get up to. Having read a fair spread of the competition I could judge exactly what I aimed to do. If I was going to break any rules or taboos, I'd know what they were and by how much I was transgressing. This knowledge is key both in terms of satisfying or disappointing your readers' expectations and in dealing with wary editors.

This kind of reading is so essential and obvious that I won't spend any more time justifying it. To write a book in a certain genre without having read other books in that genre is as impossible as building a dagoba without knowing what a dagoba is.

Factual books

Again, the usefulness of these seems self-evident. When I wrote a play set in a fictional middle-eastern country, and never having been to the Middle East, it was essential to get hold of every kind of book on that subject that I could lay my hands on. These ranged from scholarly historical and cultural works to popular guidebooks. Anything with pictures is particularly useful, as are maps.

Likewise if your character has a disease or belongs to a club or organisation or went to a certain school or college – in fact for any background detail – books are invaluable. And it's surprising how often some little fact, some habit, some custom that emerges from your book research suddenly hits you in the face and becomes an essential part of your story.

Books with a style or a voice

Imitation is an excellent way of learning. Again, the argument of 'originality' (or lack of it) is sometimes introduced here by reluctant readers. One student told me he'd had to stop reading Ernest Hemingway because he found that he'd started to write like him. My reply was, there are worse things for a learning writer than writing like Hemingway.

Struggling with a book of my own once, I stumbled across Hunter S. Thompson's magnificent *Fear and Loathing in Las Vegas*. The narrative rattles along with huge energy and apparent anarchy. Scales fell from my eyes and shackles fell from my pen. My book roared along the runway and took off. Along the way I also discovered how much careful work was required to achieve the impression of apparent spontaneity. Once my book was finished, to my knowledge only one critic spotted the influence. What I'd gained was an angle on my material and an energy I probably would never have achieved without reading Thompson's book.

Books as market research

This links closely with point (exemplary books) 1. However, rather than looking at content, you're looking at the wider issues of length, of publisher, of placement on the bookshop shelf. If you want to sell a story or novel, it makes excellent sense to know what kind of thing is being published and by whom, at what length and in what format. This kind of research is absolutely essential in some fields – for example books for younger children, where word lengths or number of pages can be very rigid.

So, there are numerous ways that reading as a writer differs from reading as a literature student:

1. There is no 'canon' of exemplary texts for creative writing. Because we are looking for things to take away and use, more than one book can give us the same thing. Therefore, expect reading lists to vary from course to course and tutor to tutor.

2. Allied to this, don't sneer at, or be surprised if tutors want you to read, 'bad' literature. If you're trying to learn what makes something work, 'bad' examples can be much more useful than good ones. Good writing often appears effortless, and the underlying techniques are skilfully concealed. In a piece of bad writing you can see just what the writer has tried to do, and it's easy to analyse why they've failed. It is also good practice to try to improve on their efforts, and make the bad piece work.

3. (My editor warned me not to say this): reading as a writer does not always entail reading a whole book from cover to cover. One of the key skills of a good writer is to go to a source and find what you want quickly, then export it in a form that you can readily transform into your work.

Of course, there are also times when you will want to read the whole book, and several books (it's always best to get more than one perspective on a subject), but in many cases you don't have to. To take our parrot example: if you find a book called *Parrots of the World: 1000 Species*, and you know that your parrot is a Columbian Blue, it doesn't make a whole lot of sense to read every word about the other 999 species. However, if you want your parrot to have certain features, you may well have to dip and skim, using the index of the book, to find one that suits your purpose. For example, for one play I needed a species of lily that flourished in the south of England, but not the north. Eventually I found one, but only after many hours perusing gardening books. It may be that for our parrot story we want one with a long beak but short wings. One of a writer's most useful skills is not only to be able to find the right book to yield this information, but also how to find the information in that book quickly.

It is important to stress that, as a writer, it would be strange indeed if you didn't enjoy reading for no specific purpose, simply out of love for the power and effects of words. After all, I don't know many musicians who don't listen to music.

So, reading as a writer is a complex and varied activity. You must be sensitive to the power and effects of words; you must be alert, prepared to analyse why some writing works and other pieces don't; you must be flexible and ready to scour a book for what you want from it. The only thing you mustn't do is to copy something word for word.

A note on plagiarism

The *Oxford English Dictionary* defines plagiarism as:

> To take and use as one's own (the thoughts, writings and inventions etc., of another person); copy (literary work, ideas, etc.) improperly or without acknowledgement.

All institutions have policies to penalise plagiarists, and most have mechanisms (electronic or otherwise) to aid in detection. It is increasingly common for a random sample of coursework to be tested for plagiarism. Penalties range from a loss of marks, through failing the assessment, to expulsion from the course.

You might argue that borrowing in creative writing is normal and even inevitable. True, all writers are influenced by other writers and borrow techniques and ideas. However, there are three points you should bear in mind if you are influenced by another writer's work:

1   You should acknowledge the debt, and reference it in a bibliography, commentary or footnote.
2   You should reflect on the nature of your borrowing, analysing what you have taken and how you have transformed it.
3   You must show that you have 'made the borrowing your own' in some significant sense.

Let's look at a couple of concrete examples (both of which actually occurred).

Student A submits a script. It has the same characters as a popular US television drama series. It has the same title as an episode from that series. The story-lines are exactly the same as the story-lines from that episode. The dialogue, while similar, is mainly paraphrased from the original. Nowhere in the submission, neither in the piece itself nor in the commentary, does student A refer to the popular television series or acknowledge any debt to it or offer any explanation of the borrowing.

Student B is a great admirer of *The Simpsons*. For his assignment he has set himself the task of analysing the structure of a *Simpsons* episode and then (using the usual characters and settings) writing an episode of his own, inventing his own story-lines, dialogue etc. His submission includes an interesting account of what he has done, including a diagrammatic break down of several 'real' *Simpsons* episodes, an analysis of the kind of audience for which the series is pitched and also some research into who actually writes the series and how they came to do it.

As I hope you will agree, the first is utterly unacceptable; the second is good writerly practice.

Speaking for myself, I will take anything I can from any other writer or artist in order to turn it into something new of my own; but by the same token, in my opinion no hell is too bad for someone to simply pass off another person's work as their own. Perhaps I'm oversensitive, but this kind of theft seems particularly offensive when it involves creative writing. Steal a history essay, you're stealing something, largely, impersonal. Steal a creative piece, you're stealing part of someone's life and experience.

Organising yourself

We've agreed that there are a lot of different kinds of work that you need to do apart from the act of writing. Just as important as doing these exercises, sketches and experiments is organising them. It's very easy to feel that these pieces of writing, because they're not fine and finished, are worthless scraps and should be hidden or thrown away. On the contrary, these materials will form the basis of your finished work and, properly organised, they will build into an impressive record of the work you've done.

Many writing courses recommend that you use a notebook or journal. In this you jot down ideas, fragments of description, interesting references, extracts from authors, in fact anything that might be useful to you as a writer.

So far so good. There remain a number of practical questions. Physically, what kind of book are you going to use? Some people like a large, scrapbook-sized volume, others a post-it-sized pad. Do you want a rough-looking thing, with rip-out and throwaway pages, or a magnificent hard-covered binding with vellum paper? How are you going to tote it around? Will it fit in a pocket, or will you have to make special efforts to transport it? How convenient will it be to use? And how confident will you be pulling it out in public?

Once you've got it going, how are you going to make best use of it? Here I have a confession to make: I use notebooks. I have shelves full of them. Most of them are reporter-size or smaller. I'm certain that they're brim full of good and interesting stuff. The trouble is, I very rarely look at them.

For the purposes of this section, I've opened one of them, at random. What do I find?

> *I'm kneeling on the floor, bare knees, shorts.*
> *The cooker's on metal feet. It's winter,*
> *Sunday, gloomy. Can't play outside.*
> *'Do some colouring.'*
> *Special books, kept on a high shelf for wet days.*

This has promise, it's interesting, but the fact is that I wrote it in 1997 and haven't looked at it since. There's been a breakdown in my communication system with myself.

In another notebook I find, scrawled across a whole page: 'Then later have you been talking to Mary'. What does this mean? I don't know. To what does it refer? I don't know that either. Who is Mary? Pass. Is it useful to me now? Not in any obvious way.

Does this mean keeping a notebook is a waste of time? No, I don't think so. The old saying goes, 'You don't know what you think until you've written it down'. By keeping a notebook, you're developing a writer's way of looking at the world, whether or not you use the things you note.

However, it would be even better if you could find a way of referencing your notebook-style musings and feeding them into your work. The following is a slightly improved and idealised version of my own 'system'.

I use scraps of paper and a voice recorder to record my spur-of-the-moment ideas, fragments of overheard conversation, inexplicable inspirations, sudden enlightenments about ongoing projects etc. I 'empty' the voice recorder every day, either entering the material in ongoing project files, or on more scraps of paper. These scraps I pile up on my desk. Every so often I get so sick of the mess that I am forced to read through them and decide whether to throw them away or keep them, or to incorporate them into an ongoing project.

I also keep a project log. This is a small hardback book, rather like an account book. Every time I have an idea, which is formed enough to call a project, I enter it in the ledger. As it develops I make a note of what stage it's at, right up to submission (and acceptance or rejection). Thus a quick flick through the ledger keeps me both up to date with where I am with various pieces of work and also reminds me of ideas that have stalled for whatever reason. I also found, when starting out, that this account-style ledger made me feel much more professional and organised. And it forces you to think at an early stage about the long-term possibilities of an idea: is it a story, a poem or a play? Might it form part of a novel? How should you go about following it up and developing it?

Each project also has a drop file in a filing cabinet where I store the scraps of paper and other research materials, long-hand experiments and structural analyses, most often in the form of diagrams.

Each project also has a computer file (and may have more than one as it progresses, see The naming of files in Chapter 7).

I don't offer this as a model solution, but I do urge you to try to find some system of storing your ideas and research and tracking projects. The main point is that you should be seeing the world as a writer all the time, and have a system whereby fleeting ideas can be recorded, combined and mulled so that perhaps they will get a chance to grow into something worthwhile over time. One thing is certain: if you don't write an idea down straightaway, however brilliant it is, you'll forget it.

Summary

- However worthwhile and stimulating your workshop sessions are, you are going to have to do the majority of your work away from the workshop. This can be difficult, given the nature of the subject and the views of it held by the people around you.
- You will have to find a place, or places, where you feel comfortable writing, and also set aside time for writing.
- You should be prepared to do a lot of work outside the actual act of writing, namely experiment, analysis and research.
- You should do a lot of reading, not only for pleasure but for a variety of practical reasons. For example, background research, market research, genre research and stylistic exemplars.
- You should be clear about what you are using from other writers, and how you are making it your own; simply taking the words of another writer and passing them off as your own is totally unacceptable.

- You should try to establish a system of notebooks, files, computer files etc. that allows you both to record ideas and to access them easily.
- You should take yourself and your writing seriously.

7

Writing and editing

- Writing: where do I start?
- What's meant by editing?
- When should I edit my work?
- How much should I edit?

How do you write?

So, at last, you're ready to start actual writing. About time too, you may say. You have files, hard or computer, which contain sketches, plans, experiments in shape and in style. There may be character analyses, background research into subject matter or location. Thus armed, you should feel confident that you can make informed decisions about how to start your piece. And also reassured that if you choose the wrong place it will not be a disaster, just another experiment from which you will learn something.

And, it may be worth stressing, you shouldn't ask too much of yourself. If through a combination of inspiration and hard work you happen to produce an original, finished masterpiece, fine, but don't insist on this level of accomplishment as the norm. You're learning and so should not expect (or be expected) to produce work of outstanding originality, at least not early on in a course.

It is enough, to start with, to define the form of the piece you want to write, to feel out its shape, to understand what kind of audience you are writing for and then produce a piece that adheres to that definition. This is how music composition students work: you should understand form and structure before you are expected to display originality. To be honest, I find students often produce their most original work when relieved of the burden of *trying* to be original.

So, you know where you're going to start, and who it's about and have some idea of what's going to happen, and also the kind of narrative position you're taking, but, physically, how do you go about it?

You have two main choices: to write in long-hand, or work directly onto a computer. Some writers prefer one method, some the other. For some (like Laurie Lee, author of *Cider with Rosie*), the feel of soft lead pencil on paper gives a sensuous delight; for others using a cheap biro makes the task seem less 'official', final and intimidating. For others – myself included – handwriting is tiring and slow compared to typing: I simply can't keep up with myself (when ideas are flowing, anyway). Even if you handwrite, unless you aim to complete your piece and then (in the manner of a nineteenth-century novelist) pass it on to a secretary to type up, you will have to transfer it to the word processor at some stage. The question then becomes, at what stage do you commit the work to electronic form? Closely allied with this decision is how you are going to edit your work.

The necessity of editing

I never change what I write because what I write is what I think, so if you change it it's like lying.

I didn't have to revise my piece because it was based on real life.

Both these quotes come from first-year creative writing students. Both make the assumption that the writer is capable of always and exactly saying what she or he wants to say first time. This is, as we've observed before, about as likely as a tin whistle player picking up a clarinet and sailing through a Mozart concerto without practice. Put baldly, if you write something, and read it over, and can't see any way of improving it, either you are the fabled untaught genius (in which case why are you on the course?) or you're deceiving yourself.

The writer who never revises is like the builder who tries to build a cathedral (or a dagoba) by tossing a few bricks, perhaps a fragment of a plan, out of the window of a moving van. Occasionally the bits may happen to fall into some kind of shape; but it is unlikely – especially if no workers are employed for the construction process – that a cathedral (or dagoba) will result.

So, however much 'training' you've done for the main writing event, it is extremely unlikely that as you begin to write, the words you use will be the best ones, or that the piece will be in the best order, will include all the incidents that need to be there and will have nothing included that could fruitfully be cut. In short, you will have to do some editing. The question is, what kind of editing, and when.

Levels of editing: how to edit, and when

Some writers, like the late Kingsley Amis, write only a small number of words per day, and edit these as they go, so that by the end of the day they are, to all intents and purposes, complete, as they will appear in the finished book. Other writers prefer to get through to the end of a rough draft before even looking at it. This avoids premature self-censorship and gives the satisfying sense of a large completed thing (however imperfect) upon which one can work. Yet others steer a middle course, reading through what they've written to get a sense of direction but not doing too much editing until they get to the end or grind to a halt.

At this point we'd better be clear about what we mean by editing. One very common (and often disastrous) model of the editing process is a slight (and often reluctant) modification of the 'I start at the beginning, end at the end and never revise' approach. It goes something like this: you get the idea, you start writing, you get to the end and then you go through your text looking for 'better' words and more 'colourful' phrases. You 'polish' your text. This polishing kind of copy-editing is necessary but is only one type of editing. Normally it should only be undertaken at a very late stage in the writing process. Why? Because editing is not a simple and exact science; it involves not only *tactical* considerations (like words, phrases, sentence length) but also *strategy*, such as narrative position, tone, characters, key events, order of events, starting point, ending point (among others). In short, there are more general questions you need to ask before you anguish over whether the sky on page seven should be 'blue' or 'azure'.

Writing any piece of work is like a journey to an unknown destination. You plan and equip yourself as best you can, but however often you read your compass you can never be quite sure that you're not going up a blind valley or getting lured into an impassable desert.

Getting on and keeping on track is the first and most important aspect of editing. So my advice is, before you start close editing of words and phrases, ask larger questions, such as:

- Is this telling the story I want to tell?
- Is each event, each passage, necessary or desirable for the telling of that story?
- Have I started in the best place?
- Are the right characters in the right place at the right time?
- Why do the characters do what they do?
- Why is the story happening now?

Whether you ask these questions as you go along, or day by day, or paragraph by paragraph is up to you, but I would suggest that it makes sense to find out whether a passage is going to be included in the final draft before you expend a lot of energy polishing it.

There are dangers with any method of working. If you write a full draft right through without any editing or thought about direction you will get a sense of satisfaction from having the raw material, but you may also find that you've gone way off track, maybe at an early stage, and so have to jettison most of what you've written and try to pick the journey up again from somewhere in the middle.

If you edit carefully as you go along, you may agonise so long over a single word that you lose the forward motion or interest in the project as a whole; or worse, the bit you are working on may not actually fit in with the piece as a whole. So you will have wasted your time, rather in the manner of someone agonising over the interior décor of a house due for demolition the following day. And close editing does tend to wed us to our work. When you've spent an hour at this kind of editing your investment in what you've written becomes too great to consider easily radical changes or omissions, and so the house that should be bulldozed remains standing.

As a student of creative writing you need to understand not just that editing is a necessary part of the writing process but also that there are different levels of editing, appropriate at different stages of the development of a piece of work. It is, again, up to you to find a way of working that best keeps you on track.

Too Much for Normous

Perhaps a case study from my own experience will illustrate the different levels of editing more clearly.

I was fortunate that my first book for young people was picked off the 'slush pile' at the first publishing house to which I sent it. However, the editor there didn't immediately congratulate me on my genius and offer me vast sums of money; she asked me to meet her and she pointed out some structural weaknesses that she felt needed attention, namely the ordering of certain events and the function of certain characters. She made no comments (and I stress this) about individual words or passages. All her advice was general and structural (and very good).

I took her advice and made structural changes. Now the big cheque? No; she still had to sell the book within her company to the editorial board, which also involved marketing people. She came back with more feedback; namely that two chapters were inappropriately written from the parents' (rather than the children's) point of view, and the end was too gloomy. I considered the feedback and made further changes. It still took my editor nearly a year of persistence to convince the editorial board to take a chance on the book. At last she reported back the good news, that they would take it and publish it.

Now the champagne and fortune? Not quite; she said that first she'd send me my manuscript marked up with her editorial suggestions. It was only at this stage that she started the close reading, copy-editing process. I include one page from that manuscript, marked up by her. The square brackets indicate things she thought should be cut (incidentally, she was absolutely right); in the margin she has given the reason (or one of the reasons): 'too authorial'. In other words the voice of the author was intruding too much on the characters and the story.

She hadn't confronted me with this devastating close editing until (a) the structure had been taken care of, and (b) the book had been bought. That is the mark of a very good editor; as, incidentally, was her withholding until the latest possible moment the one final and absolute condition imposed by the editorial board – that I change the cringe-making title.

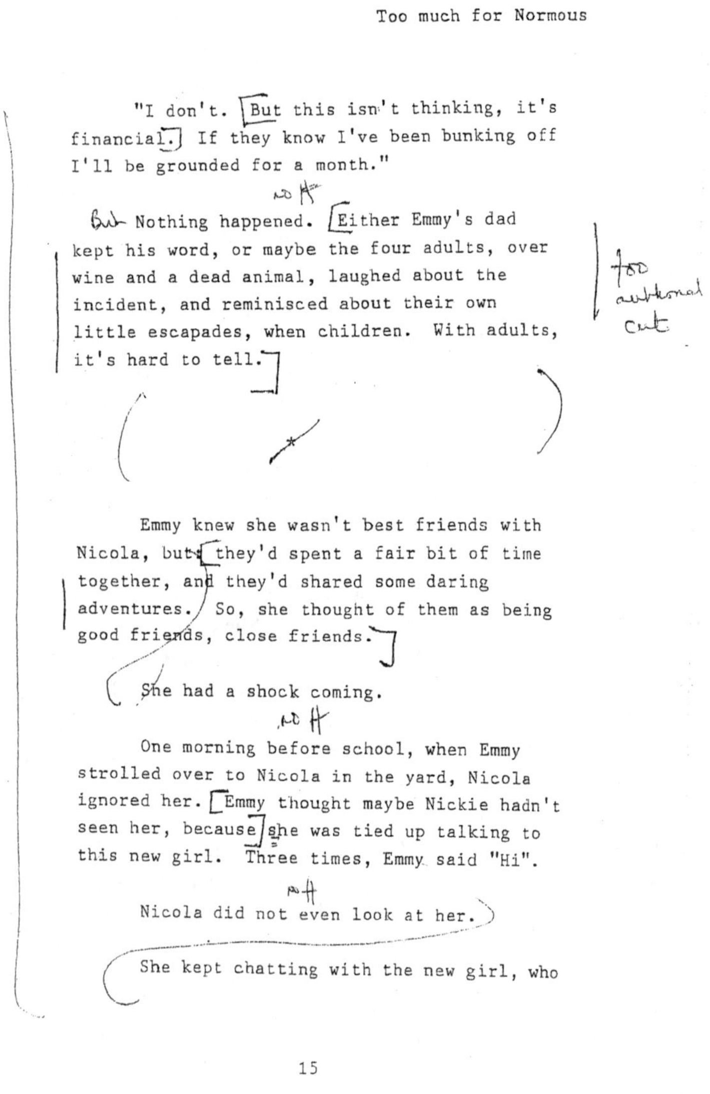

Too much for Normous

"I don't. [But this isn't thinking, it's
financial.] If they know I've been bunking off
I'll be grounded for a month."

~~But~~ Nothing happened. [Either Emmy's dad
kept his word, or maybe the four adults, over
wine and a dead animal, laughed about the
incident, and reminisced about their own
little escapades, when children. With adults,
it's hard to tell.]

Too
additional
cut

Emmy knew she wasn't best friends with
Nicola, but they'd spent a fair bit of time
together, and they'd shared some daring
adventures. So, she thought of them as being
good friends, close friends.]

She had a shock coming.

One morning before school, when Emmy
strolled over to Nicola in the yard, Nicola
ignored her. [Emmy thought maybe Nickie hadn't
seen her, because/she was tied up talking to
this new girl. Three times, Emmy said "Hi".

Nicola did not even look at her.)

She kept chatting with the new girl, who

15

Figure 7.1 **My editor's copy-editing of a script**

Perhaps the chief aim of any writing course is to make you a better editor of your own work, knowing when to apply the different levels of editing necessary to get a play, book, poem or story into the best possible shape.

The naming of files

Editing may be primarily concerned with artistic or aesthetic considerations, but there's a very important nuts-and-bolts aspect to editing too. You as a student of creative writing need to know what level of editing to apply at each stage of the writing process, but also how to handle those levels of editing in terms of hard-copy drafts and computer files.

Probably most of us have had the sickening experience of revising a piece, apparently saving it, only to find, when we return to it, the old unrevised version. Likewise, many of us will have spent long hours revising a piece of work only to find we weren't working on the most up-to-date version. In one extreme case I found that, for whatever reason (presumably human error on my own or my editor's part), a whole chapter appeared in the proofs of a novel in its ancient, pre-edited, form. Fortunately, I did have the most up-to-date version on my computer.

But, you may ask, why have you got more than one version of a piece? Surely you just keep the one file with the one name. Why save old versions? I save old versions because I find it helps me make big editorial decisions. For example, if I want to cut a large section, or move large parts, such decisions might be disastrous, and so I like to have the old version there as a long stop, a point to return to.

My advice (which I don't always stick to myself) is to name files in a clear way that will show you at a glance which is the most recent. I will usually try to give this file the basic name of the piece, for example my play Chess Wars is called 04chess (04 because that's the year I was writing it). I have various directories for various kinds of work, for example stories, radio and TV. 04chess is stored in my radio directory, because it's a radio play. If I was to try to adapt it for television, I'd store that version in the TV directory. I'd suggest that you, likewise, set up directories for each unit or module that you study, for ease of finding relevant experiments, research, drafts and notes.

If I look back in my files, I find files called 03chess (because I started working on the play in 2003), and also 04chessold (an old version from which I substantially departed for the subsequent drafts). There are also files called 04chessol1 and chessol2. It would take me a little investigation into the properties of these files to find out when they branched off from the main working file, and why. I hope I never have to carry out that investigation. However, these files might be useful if I want to find a section or speech that I cut from the working file. For example, I'm currently adapting *Chess Wars* for a German production. The German director wants to highlight political elements – elements that I researched and drafted but cut from the English version. I can now find these and reinstate them.

I only rename a draft at crucial editing stages. During normal editing, if I cut a section I simply paste it at the end of the current working version, so it's handy if I change my mind.

The script will be edited further during rehearsal, and though I mark up these changes on a hard copy of the script, unless the script is going to be published, I don't then go home and copy them to my electronic files – which is probably laziness.

One final suffix I have used twice (but didn't have to with Chess Wars) is 'des', as in one called 03mendes in my children's book directory. 'des' stands for desperation, when I have written so many unsuccessful drafts of a book that I cannot bear to keep counting them. 'des' means do or die, now or never, ready or not, what the hell is this all about?, give me a break. On both occasions it seemed to work, but I can't be sure it always will, or that it will work for you.

I don't, in any sense, offer this system (insofar as it is a system) as a perfect model. Other writers work differently, and probably with more efficiency. The main thing is to develop a system where you can find what you want and know which file to work on. The great danger lies in getting confused about which is your most up-to-date version of a piece of work, and hence doing edits at different times on two or more different versions, so that you end up with a hopeless mess.

Task avoidance

After all this preparation and research, experiment and analysis, with a private space and a blank sheet of paper, and a full day, or half-day set aside from other commitments, what happens if you can't write any-thing? Setting aside a block of time can also be daunting. What happens if you don't get 'inspired'? The clock ticks on, your mind is a blank, and there's *Supermarket Sweep* on the television, Freecell on the computer.

Well, we already have one answer: there are lots of things you could do apart from the big W. You could experiment, analyse or research. You could read other books. You could go to the bookshop and have a look at other things written in a similar genre to that which you're attempting. You could visit a place where your work is set, and make notes. You could check bus timetables or theatre programmes. You could just take your notebook or voice recorder for a walk and hope that you can strike up a dialogue.

If you're not going to do any of those things, if you insist on sitting at your desk with a blank mind and blank sheet, well, let's face it, it's not that you *can't* work, the fact is you *won't*. You just can't motivate yourself to get started. Let's be brutal, you are being lazy.

I can say this without embarrassment, because most writers are masters of task avoidance, and I am no exception. I find it easy to avoid working, both when I'm stuck on a project and, perhaps paradoxically, even more so when it's going wonderfully well. There's nothing better than the sense of joy and power derived from knowing that you have a strong section of a piece to write, you know in your blood what's going to happen, you are alive with anticipation; and you do every other thing in the world but actually sit down and write it.

Jack London (author of *Call of the Wild*) probably liked a drink more than was good for him (he died of liver failure). However, he did use this predilection positively for his work. He would make himself write one thousand words before he took his first drink of the day. Normally he was downing his scotch and soda by around 10.15a.m.

While I by no means recommend this exact method of self-motivation, I do advocate self-bribery. This is how I try and reduce the intimidation of the blank page and a long, blank day. I make myself work for five minutes, just five minutes, with the promise of a reward afterwards (a walk, a glance at *Sunset Beach*, a cup of coffee). If you keep making yourself do this, over a period you will accumulate a body of raw material to work on. And sometimes, if you get absorbed in your work, that five minutes can turn into fifty, or five hours.

The key thing is the effort of will required to start working. If you say you can't think of anything to write, well write anything, write nonsense, write out a shopping list, write a diary entry.

When it comes down to it, task avoidance is both an occupational hazard for a writer and inexcusable. There are always things you can do. At least be honest and confront the reasons behind your reluctance to work. Try not to take refuge in empty appeals to lack of inspiration or block. Because if you really can't think of anything to write, or anything to research, any relevant analysis, background reading or things to experiment with, maybe you're doing the wrong course and ought to simply admit it and quit, and do something else where the necessary levels of self-direction and self-motivation are lower.

Word counts again

After our excursion through all the other things a writer needs to do in order to write effectively, all the background reading, research, experimentation, drafting, revising and editing, the word count will, in fact, seem dauntingly *small* to convey the range and depth of your study. You will be forced to select carefully from a much wider range of work than you are formally allowed to submit.

The few thousand words of your submission are a chance for you not only to display to the reader (in this case marker) a sequence of more or less well-put-together words on a page, but also to open a window on the full range and depth of your work for the course. So, as the haiku evokes in its 17 syllables worlds beyond those mere words, your limited word count is a chance to present an illustrative and evocative sample of your achievement.

To help you convey the range of your study you may be allowed (sometimes encouraged or forced) to submit appendices, consisting of old drafts, drawings for a stage play set, research notes for a historical story, character sketches etc. Make the most of these opportunities. If you've read a lot of books, make sure you append a full bibliography, properly presented. In short, if you've done a lot, flaunt it: make sure your reader knows just how much work you've done.

It might help to bear in mind that your submissions are very similar to a writer's 'selling documents', for example the kind of package a television writer has to put together when trying to sell a series. He or she can't submit the whole series fully written (even if they've written it); what they must do is put together an outline, a treatment, a synopsis, character sketches, along with *some* script, to indicate the full range and nature of the project. And the whole package will be severely limited in terms of size. Paradoxically, the smaller the word count, the harder it is to put together an effective submission.

And believe me, there is a huge difference between reading a single draft, 'struggle for the finishing line' piece of work, and something that has been researched, honed, revised and shaped with the intention of showing off the full range of a student's knowledge and achievement. That difference will be reflected in your grades.

Presentation and layout: make your work a pleasure to read

So, you've done the work, you've written the assignment and you've edited it through all the stages. The piece of work is 'ready to go'. Job done? Not quite. For any writer (unless you're writing purely for your own private purposes) a central concern is getting people to read your work. If you're trying to sell your work, your first target is an industry professional, for example an agent or a script editor. These are busy people who are, by and large, looking for reasons *not* to read the vast amount of unsolicited material that comes their way. Many publishers in fact refuse to read unsolicited material at all.

What's all this to you? You're a student and someone is being *paid* to read and mark your work. Yes, but they too are busy, they too are human; they will not necessarily have the patience to penetrate crumpled and creased pages, spelling mistakes or badly formatted text in order to grasp your inner meaning.

An exercise I use is this. I show students a sample of past coursework submissions. We don't read them, or even find out what the subject matter is; all we look at is the 'packaging' and presentation. I ask students to grade the submissions based solely on this information. They are surprised to find that the grades they award, based entirely on presentation, very often (though not always) correlate closely with the marks awarded for the pieces as a whole. But is it any surprise that people who take most care over presentation have also done the same with the content?

Writers are often and rightly urged to get a 'hook' near the beginning of a piece, but the best hook in the world is useless if it never gets near the mouth of the fish. Hooks usually need bait; and, put crudely, if your presentation annoys, fatigues or otherwise puts the fish off, you might as well not have bothered. A producer who rejected an early script of mine did so on the (wholly justified) basis that I hadn't laid it out according to proper conventions: 'I can't read that,' he said, 'it just doesn't look like a script.'

So make sure you have got your content 'hook' enticingly baited, in the presentation itself. An analogy is trying to sell a flat or house. As you may have gathered from many popular television programmes, it isn't the essence of a house that sells but the impression it makes on the buyer. I can speak from experience. Our flat wouldn't sell. Everyone said how dark it was. We bought a cheap but very bright standard lamp and a cheap white carpet for the entrance hall. After that, everyone who came to view remarked on how bright it was, and we sold it soon after. So, don't neglect presentation.

Every institution and course will have its own guidelines for presentation of submitted work, but here are some general observations that may be useful. Starting negatively, basic presentational errors to avoid (and most of these are equally applicable to academic or professional submissions):

- omission of official coversheet;
- mis-spelling of recipient/marking tutor's name;
- wrong title for recipient (especially if you carelessly downgrade them);
- wrong module number/course title/assignment title;
- staples, especially if badly administered;
- crumpled and creased pages;
- coffee or wine stains, glass rings, encrusted food;
- inaccessibility of pages (especially if each page is prisoned in a separate plastic envelope);
- elaborate binding;
- tiny typeface;
- huge typeface;
- unconventional typeface (unless you have very good reasons, which you should make clear);
- smeary typeface;
- huge blocks of unbroken text;
- inexplicable line breaks;
- absence of page numbering;
- inconsistent page numbering;
- inconsistent or non-existent paragraphing conventions;
- inconsistent or non-existent speech conventions.

As with most things to do with writing, there is no definitive right way of doing things that, if slavishly followed, will yield results, but here are some positive guidelines in terms of presentation:

- space your work (1.5 or double);
- leave generous margins;
- split your text up into paragraphs;
- find a way of holding the whole together that is both smart, secure, yet easy to access (I prefer some variation of the slip-on spine);
- be extra careful about the cover sheet and the first couple of pages;
- make sure you label your work with the right course or module code and title; and
- get the name of your tutor right.

In short, make your submission a pleasure to see and to handle, so that your reader will want to read it.

Summary

- You should experiment with means of writing (pen, pencil, straight onto computer) to find out what suits you best.
- You should be aware of different levels of editing and when to apply them.
- You should try to develop a system for the clear naming of files.
- Word counts in assessment items are not a finishing line to be reached and then forgotten, but a restricted opportunity to show the huge wealth and breadth of work you've done in a unit.
- Task avoidance is a common problem for writers, but there's no excuse not to work. There's plenty to do apart from the actual writing.
- And when you come to submit your work, make it a pleasure for your marker to read.

Conclusion

Beyond the course

- What will a creative writing degree qualify me for?
- Can I go on studying?
- How do I go about carrying on writing?

This final section gives you a broad picture of the avenues open to you after completing a course in or involving creative writing. The main thing is for you to decide what you really want to do and then take positive steps to achieve those aims.

Had enough?

You may have tried doing creative writing and decided it isn't for you. That in itself is no bad outcome; there are too many people who harbour an untried (and probably unrealistic) longing to write. If you have tried, and can reflect on your experience and analyse why you don't want to pursue writing further, you will have learned a great deal, both about writing and about yourself.

Furthermore, if your course has been a good course, and you've made best use of it, you should have a fairly clear idea of how 'creative industries' work, and how work gets sold. You should also, more generally, have learned how to manage a project from initial idea through to completion, and to work with other people in a flexible, supportive and intelligent way. These aren't insignificant accomplishments; they should equip you well, whatever direction you decide to take.

For example, a recent graduate phoned me to let me know that she'd got the job she wanted, working with young people. The selection process had involved several dozen applicants who were split up into small groups, asked to discuss the issues involved in the job and then asked to write a report on those discussions. Our creative writing graduate got the job because apart from her personal qualities, she had spent three years in small groups discussing issues and writing pieces based on those discussions.

However, if you haven't had enough of doing creative writing, what options do you have? At the end of this section you'll find eight case studies, all but one of whom did creative writing in one form or another. You will see the varied career paths that they've followed, united only by two things: the difficulty, even after being published, of earning a living as a writer; and their continuing commitment and determination to write.

The academic route: further study

A growing number of institutions offer creative writing courses at MA level and beyond. The variety of origins and development of creative writing is apparent at these levels too. Whereas in long-established subjects like History or English there will be an accepted and logical articulation between undergraduate and postgraduate study, this is not necessarily the case with creative writing.

Perhaps the most obvious indicator of this absence of articulation is the fact that there's not a single MA Creative Writing course (certainly in the UK) that demands an undergraduate writing degree as a condition of entry. This might seem bizarre, especially if we compare it to the situation in other subjects – surely you'd need a first degree in, say, psychology before you could embark on a Psychology Master's?

Generally speaking, entry to MA courses is dependent on commitment to writing, evidence of (some) talent, and ability to pay. Experience of those reflective, academic aspects of doing creative writing at under-graduate level – the contextualising of what you write and analysis of process – are not generally required. This will be good news if you've only done a small amount of creative writing within another degree programme and want to do more. However, if most Master's level students don't have the undergraduate qualification, this will have a large bearing on the kind of people you are studying with.

At my own institution the chief 'market' for the MA is not graduating BA students. Out of 40–50 MA students each year, only two or three will move directly on from the BA to the MA programme. The bulk of the MA cohort is made up of more mature students who haven't done a first degree in writing. It would be fair to say that for most of them their main concern is to get published, not to get a degree, nor to study a subject.

This may suit you, if your main aim is to land a six-figure, two-book deal. However, such emphasis is less satisfactory in the larger context of the growth and definition of creative writing as a subject.

For example, if you are one of the growing number of people who, having done creative writing and want to go on and teach it, then although you'll want an MA programme orientated towards the 'real' world, you'll also want a reflective academic element that contextualises the writing and equips you to teach with more authority than is given by the simple fact of having written, and possibly published, something. The US has two kinds of Master's-level degrees in writing, which perhaps serves to emphasise this distinction. The Master of Arts tends to combine elements of literature and writing, as opposed to the MFA (Master of Fine Arts), which is a terminal, studio, practice-based degree.

So before applying to do an MA, I'd recommend that you decide what you want out of it, and then do some research to find out exactly what each MA programme actually offers.

There are now a number of institutions in the UK, the US and Australia offering PhDs in creative writing, but at the time of writing I think it's fair to say that progression from BA through MA to PhD is still not transparent and consistent across the sector, and the best ways of integrating creative to critical elements in the PhD are still being thrashed out. However, the future evolution of creative writing as a subject is going to depend significantly on the input of people doing PhDs. So, if your first course has enthused you to pursue your studies as far as you can, by studying at doctoral level you will be taking part in an exciting period of development and definition.

Writing

There is no standard career structure for creative writers. There are too many writers looking for too little work. It is not enough to write well; you must be prepared to sell your work, and yourself, and, incidentally, have a good measure of luck. But to go back to our golfing analogy, it's hardly surprising that the more you try, the more chances you give yourself of being lucky.

If you want to keep writing, the most important thing is to keep writing. Practice is no less important at the end of a degree programme than at the beginning. Yes, you will have gained lots of knowledge, understanding and skills, but unless you continually use those skills they will go rusty and you will slide back down to somewhere near the bottom of the mountain you've climbed. As a famous pianist (Vladimir Horowitz) is said to have remarked, 'If I don't practise for a day, I know it; if I don't practise for two days, my wife knows it; and if I don't practise for three days, the world knows it'.

As you will see from our case studies, determined writers find various ways to keep writing, and keep the motivation to write. You might consider taking short courses run by colleges or by specialist organisations, or join a writing group, either 'live' or via the internet. You could also (if script is your thing) get involved in theatre groups or amateur dramatics. Whatever your favoured genre, you can look out for competitions, which are an excellent focus, with a deadline. Another good way to keep writing is to target magazines or newspapers – and this deserves a section to itself.

Journalism

If you want to be a news journalist, and you've done creative writing, then I'm afraid you probably took the wrong course (though it's not too late to top up with the necessary technical and legal knowledge and skills with an appropriate MA or Diploma course). However, feature journalism is a great area to practise, to improve your writing and to build up a portfolio of work and a publications list for your CV.

The process is fairly straightforward, but may be worth spelling out. Start with magazines you read yourself. For example, if you're into fly fishing, do you read *Fly Fishing Monthly* (if there is such a thing)? Have a closer look at it. Are there articles by freelance writers? Is there some small print somewhere near the contents page that either invites or discourages unsolicited submissions? If they do take unsolicited pieces, do they have a standard word length? If this is not specified, analyse the articles in the current edition to work it out. Also analyse the content of the articles – are they information-based or anecdotal; do they sometimes deal with historical aspects of the sport? Also, is there a house style (jokey, serious, practical, whimsical, personal etc.)? Finally, who is the person who is responsible for buying freelance contributions (very important – remember your training in submitting coursework).

If the magazine does take freelance contributions, I suggest you practise a couple of times writing pieces to fit the brief of the publication in question, then when you feel confident enough that you can do the job, make contact with the person responsible for buying contributions. Do it by phone or by e-mail. Be pleasant, be sensitive, be business-like. If the person is clearly stressed and pushed for time, try to get them to suggest a better time to call back. When you have cornered them, tell them what you have on offer and ask if they're interested. If they're not interested, ask if there's anything else they might be looking for.

Be pleasant and politely persistent. Show an understanding of their (inexplicable) rejection of your last 30 suggestions. Keep coming up with new ideas, new angles and keep offering them. Eventually, if only out of pity or frustration, if your writing is good enough, they will crack, and commission you.

I've used rather aggressive terms like 'cornered', 'target' and 'crack', but what you're aiming for is to get on good terms with the editor/commissioner, so that when they hear your voice on the other end of the phone they don't cringe but breathe a sigh of relief, pleased that they have someone sensible and pleasant to talk to. In this connection it can do you no harm whatever to indulge in a little mild flattery, especially if that flattery also demonstrates your intimate knowledge of their particular publication. So, for example, an opening gambit such as the following could be worth trying:

> Yes, I never miss *Fly Fishing Monthly,* and I was ringing to say how much I enjoyed the series of articles on Portuguese twisted hemp lures. They were mind blowing. And then it struck me; I wondered if you'd be interested in something similar on Sardinian carp-sensitive . . .

You also aim to show that you are resourceful, flexible and reliable. You're not a street-corner match-seller with only one product; you're more like a sleight-of-hand balloon-bender – if they don't want your creation shaped like a dog, how about you turn it into a giraffe?

If you do reach the stage with an editor that they rate you as resourceful, flexible and reliable, they will eventually start ringing you with ideas and projects, and also passing your name on to others in the industry.

Books

Compared with short-feature journalism, writing a full-length book is a long-drawn-out and lonely process. However, a lot of the networking habits outlined in the Journalism section above are equally applicable to a beginning novelist.

There is an oft-quoted saying that if your writing is good enough it will eventually get published, and maybe that's true, but why not optimise your chances? We've seen that in the writing of a piece, throwing bricks out of a moving van window is hardly likely to make a cathedral; similarly, throwing your finished cathedral out of a moving van window is unlikely to 'place' it where it's best suited to be.

So, analyse the market, find out which agents deal with which kinds of writing, and which publishers publish which books. If you can make personal contact before sending your manuscript, all the better, so long as you're sensitive and intelligent about what you have to sell. If you can get them to *ask you* to see your work, you'll stand a much better chance of getting your book considered seriously than if you just stick the manuscript in an envelope with a covering letter.

If you do sell a book, it is not certain or likely that the advance you're given will be enough to live on, or recompense you for the amount of work you've put in. A relative of mine harboured desires to be a novelist and asked me about remuneration. When I (rather proudly) told him the amount of my previous advance he shook his head in pitying wonder, with the words, 'I wouldn't get out of bed for that'.

A recent Society of Authors survey in the UK showed that only a tiny proportion of members earned more than £20,000 a year, while the vast majority would happily settle for that figure. This figure compares to an average annual wage in the UK at the time of writing of around £25,000.

Even if, like one of our graduates, you get £120,000 for a two-book deal, when you start to cost it out, that won't come in at much more than

£40,000 a year if each book takes 18 months to write. And if you boil it down to an hourly rate, less research expenses, the figures can become less than attractive. Which is, I suppose, just another way of saying, the only worthwhile reason for writing is wanting to write. Fame and fortune are probably gained more reliably elsewhere.

Scriptwriting

Scriptwriting, especially for television, is probably the most reliable form of earning decent regular money for writers at the moment. Rates vary for beginners and established writers, and depend on the status of the programme for which they are writing, but an episode for a popular soap opera in the UK should earn you between £3,000 and £5,000, which isn't bad for what should only be a week or so's work.

Having said that, television writing is extremely hard to break into, and if you do want to break in you are probably going to be starting with lower-rated and lower-paid daytime soaps. The days of single original plays, of experimental dramatists like Dennis Potter, are, for better or worse, gone, probably for good. If you write for television you will have to write as part of a team, probably using other people's characters, situations and story-lines, at least to start with.

In the UK there is still a large market for radio drama. Radio is easier to get started in than television (though it's getting harder for someone with no track record in another medium). It pays about half of what TV does, and does still offer some opportunities for original drama, though the commissioners have very clear ideas about what they want for particular slots.

Theatre is still the place for original plays, but don't expect to earn very much. You may not make the West End or Broadway first time off, but there are lots of amateur dramatic societies looking for plays. Again, go and see what's on, look out for local groups, competitions and schemes. Visit local professional theatres and sound out their policy on new writing. Showing people that you're interested in theatre will make them more likely to be interested in you.

Poetry

If you want to make a fortune out of writing, becoming a poet is not a smart option. However, the same kind of networking that we explored in the Journalism section is required, to get your name, face and, eventually, poems known in the right quarters. Research where poetry appears, and what kind of poetry. Then there's always the performance option, if you've got the bottle.

Whatever your genre, sitting at home and waiting for the world to recognise your unpublished genius is about as effective a career plan as sitting in front of a blank computer screen waiting for inspiration to write the book in the first place.

And if you can't get published yet, then the next best thing is to find work in a related industry.

Writing-related careers

If, after your course finishes, you want to carry on writing, the chances are that you will, certainly to start with, have to work at something else in order to earn a living. If you are going to have to earn a living doing something other than writing, then it does seem to make sense to sound out work in what are broadly known as the *creative industries*.

Many established novelists started work in publishing houses or working for agents or advertising agencies; playwrights have worked in theatres as stage or front-of-house managers, and likewise television and radio writers doing various jobs in the broadcast industries. Again, and going back to our remarks about networking above, this is not rocket science. Knowing publishers and editors isn't going to be a disadvantage when you start trying to sell your novel; neither is it a disadvantage to have first-hand knowledge of the way the television industry works when you come to peddle your sitcom.

And finally . . .

Whatever direction you decide to take after doing creative writing, I wish you every success. In the next chapter are some real-life examples of what can happen to you after doing creative writing.

Case studies

James Joyce and other writers

I've started these case studies with James Joyce because I want to emphasise that this most celebrated of writers was no different from any other writer in terms of the way his books got written. *Ulysses* did not spring fully formed from his head; it was the result of a complex process and involved solving a wide variety of problems, both internal to the book and external (such as finance).

James Joyce (1882–1941), author of *Dubliners, A Portrait of the Artist as a Young Man, Ulysses* and *Finnegans Wake,* didn't do a degree in creative writing; nor did he quickly or easily become successful and earn a living from his writing.

He had a variety of jobs, some of them writing-related. He was a sub-editor for a beekeeping journal (for about a day) and wrote reviews for a paper (until the editor told him his contributions were no longer required). He also taught, though latterly his students became more like patrons, giving him money for lessons they never expected to receive. Joyce's brother Stanislaus was for many years a ready and willing source of money and support, although later he became disillusioned with his brother's profligacy and heavy drinking.

For a while Joyce worked in a bank in Trieste. He hated the business suit and the regular hours. He also tried his hand as an entrepreneur, acting as agent for the setting up of a cinema in Dublin.

Perhaps of most use to Joyce were women of a certain background and substance, for example Sylvia Beach (proprietor of the famous Shakespeare and Co. bookshop in Paris), who eventually published *Ulysses*, and Harriet Weaver, who gave financial support (at first anonymous) to the tune, in modern terms, of £500,000 or more. This was to aid with the writing of his major 'Work in Progress' through the 1920s and 1930s, which was eventually published as *Finnegans Wake*, and which Harriet Weaver hated.

Although his published output was relatively small, throughout his life, and despite bad trouble with his eyesight, Joyce worked hard and regularly at his writing. His partner, family and friends came second to his work. He refused to compromise in terms of content, a refusal that delayed the publication of *Dubliners* for ten years.

What does all this mean to you, as a student of creative writing? That you should be offered modules in Obtaining Rich Sponsors, or The Consequences of Sticking to Your Principles without Compromise? Perhaps not, in such bald and exaggerated terms, but your course should make you aware of

- writing-related ways of earning money;
- the possible consequences of High Principles on your chances of publication;
- the importance of networking and knowing the right people;
- the difficulty of earning a living as a writer of any kind;
- the importance for your career of persistence and single-mindedness; and
- the dangers of persistence and single-mindedness for your personal life.

And who knows, you may decide that you quite like the idea of the job in the bank, working steady, regular hours, wearing a smart suit, and without the pressure to produce which devils a writer's life. If your course teaches you no more than that, it is a valuable lesson.

Case study 2

NS graduated in 1999. He did a joint honours degree in English and Creative Writing. 'It was a very good combination; both sides threw light on each other'. He chose the institution because of the creative writing option. One of his school teachers had been a student at the institution and recommended it to him. He'd wanted to be a writer since he was 14, when a teacher had read out something of his in class and given positive feedback. He did the degree straight from school. This did raise some problems. 'I'd been working flat out for A Levels – lunchtimes, evenings – to get the grades. There didn't seem to be much to do in the first year at uni, and the bar was very cheap. I lost momentum.'

He also felt slightly intimidated by the whole thing, coming from a background where no-one else was writing, or shared his ambition to become a writer. He didn't feel comfortable with a whole classroom of other people writing. 'Even after I'd finished the degree, a writer was always someone else, never me.'

By the time he finished, he 'didn't have a great attitude towards study. I'd gone from wanting to do it to not being that bothered.' A tutor suggested he think of journalism, so he wrote a piece (based on his mother's experiences on a company day out) and submitted it to a local paper. They didn't print it, but offered him a week's work. After that he was offered another week with a sister paper in another area, and then a permanent job.

'Writing at the paper was completely different from what I'd done at university. There was a total lack of guidance, and I didn't have a clue what to do.' He would write stories and get them returned as unsatisfactory, but with no explanation or guidance as to how to make them right. It was also hard work, starting at seven in the morning and finishing at seven at night (or later if detailed to the dreaded local council meetings).

He worked as a reporter for a year. Why did he leave? 'I couldn't stand the ethics or lack of them. You had to be prepared to do anything to get your story, and I wasn't prepared to do that. Just one example: when the paper was covering a car crash and the parents of the victims wouldn't give photos, our reporter went to the scene of the crash where the family had put flowers and pictures of the victims and he copied them. They appeared in the paper. I wasn't that type of person; I wasn't tough enough and I didn't want to be.'

He had done no writing of his own while with the paper. He started writing again while working in a Learning Support unit (a government funded school-based centre for pupils with various social or learning issues), and continued after doing a postgraduate course that enabled him to become a teacher. 'I'd do bits morning or evenings or weekends, or if I thought of something while I was driving home I'd do that when I got home before my school work.'

In 2005 his desire to write seriously resurfaced, and at the time of writing he is taking a scriptwriting MA (while still teaching at his school part-time). 'I feel now I have more to write about, more to say. The time seems right to push forward with my writing again.'

Points to consider

- You may not find every form of professional writing suits you.
- To find what you really want to write about may take considerable time and life experience.
- Fitting writing in around a full-time job is possible, but demanding.

Case study 3

As a mature student with two children, NW did a combined Creative Writing and English degree (2 to 1 in favour of creative writing). 'I've always had a strong urge to write and thought doing a degree would give me the chance to practise intensely and at the same time get feedback to find out if I was any good. I consequently became obsessed with getting a First.'

Her family background lay in the arts and culture. 'There were always books. I read voraciously.' However, prior to taking the course she'd escaped an abusive relationship where she was constantly told she was stupid.

'I had to do A Level English to get onto the course. There was a lot of support for that. With the degree it's more detached; not that that's a bad thing.'

As the course progressed NW hit upon the novel she wanted to write. 'By the end I couldn't wait for the degree to finish so I could get on with working on the book.' Graduating in 2001, she finished a rough first draft over the ensuing summer. Then came the long haul of redrafting, which was 'hard to justify to others as you're not earning anything doing it'. She also had to do a succession of menial, part-time jobs, including bar work, cooking and gardening, as well as looking after her children. 'But anything that took me away from the writing I resented.'

To keep up momentum she joined a writing group, then forming a smaller offshoot with a couple of other members, one of whom now has a London agent.

With the redrafting just over half complete, NW started trying to interest people in the book. 'By now I was really sick of it, so I sent the beginning to an agent and a publisher. Both asked to see the rest.'

The result was that NW had to write the ending in a hurry. Although the publisher was complimentary, he could not take it in the rushed state. So, NW has spent another year rewriting the book completely. Was that hard? 'Yes, but I felt, I've invested so many years, I've got to do it. Sometimes when I read it I think it's shit, other times I really enjoy it.'

At the time of writing, her manuscript is back with the publisher, awaiting his verdict.

Points to consider

- Even if you discover quite early the thing you really want to write, it can be a long and complicated process getting it written.
- Working on your own after doing a course can be difficult, especially when other people challenge your right to call yourself a writer.
- If you approach agents or publishers, make sure you've got something to sell them.

Case study 4

Beckie Williams went straight to university from school. 'It was a very academic school and I think maybe they expected me to do law or medicine or something. But I thought, if it's three years you'd better do something you really enjoy.' So she did a Creative Writing degree with a minor element of English, with no expectation of getting a job at the end of it. She was surprised to find that not all of her fellow students were as focused or motivated as herself. Some of them found the high pressure demoralising. 'Some had never shown anyone their work before and they couldn't take it. I liked that kind of pressure.'

Her experience of tutors was various. The best inspired her, gave her huge support, pushed her to produce her best work and put her in touch with people in the publishing world. Others, with whom she felt she had a 'clash of personality and taste', were not helpful at all. 'In the end I shaped my work to suit their taste. I suppose it's just being aware of your audience.'

The course didn't assist much with dealing with the 'real world', being more concerned with writing than being a writer. Of the fellow students that she keeps in touch with, only one is still writing. All the others have abandoned writing, working in a variety of jobs (advertising, the police, a pub).

Beckie's break came after a chance meeting with someone who was just starting work with a publisher. He suggested she submit some work and she sent him some old university coursework. The publisher couldn't use that but offered her the chance to write a non-fiction book for children. She is currently working on her ninth. 'When the first one was published, that was all I'd ever wanted, but then you have to reassess your goals.'

'I always wanted to write adult stuff, but now it's hard to get out of the child thing.' She is currently in touch with another (adult) publisher, reworking another piece of coursework. 'I've finally realised what I have to do to it to make it really good.'

Points to consider

- Who you know may not be more important than what you know, but knowing the right people is not a disadvantage when it comes to furthering your writing career.
- Having success in one field of writing does not guarantee success in another.
- Do one commission well, and you'll probably be offered more work.

Case study 5

Ben Cannon graduated in 2001. He chose his course because it contained a creative writing element. 'I'd wanted to be a writer ever since I was nine or ten.' He started off doing major English with minor Creative Writing, but as the course progressed he ended up majoring in creative writing. The course gave him more or less what he expected, formalising the knowledge he'd picked up writing as a hobby, and going into greater detail. He found workshops useful, both the exercises and the supportive criticism of peers and tutors, although he concedes that 'every time you read something out you are baring your soul.' He also found it very useful to have contact with tutors who were working writers and 'knew the business'.

When he left university he got a full-time job in a pension office, but kept up his writing in the evenings. Someone he knew had an idea for a novel, and Ben wrote it for them. This gave him a great sense of achievement, because it was the first long-form piece he'd finished, both using and extending what he'd learned on the undergraduate course.

He then went on a short course for theatre writers, and the tutors advised him that the best way to progress was to get involved in amateur dramatics, not necessarily as a writer, but to see how things work. By chance he met up with an ex-teacher who was involved in amateur dramatics, whom he asked, 'Do you by any chance need a writer?' She said that they were looking for an original piece for a festival. Ben took up the challenge, wrote a one-act play, and they 'picked it up and ran with it'. The play was performed in 2004 and won an award for the best original play at the festival.

'The good thing about getting it performed was that I'd proved to myself I could do it.' Accordingly, Ben went part-time at work, reserving Friday as his designated writing day. 'I was pretty disciplined, working regular hours.' He's just started experimenting with voice-recognition software, but normally develops his initial ideas longhand in a hardback notebook before transferring them to computer. 'The cursor can be rather demoralising, sitting there flashing at you, as if as to say, "Write something, I dare you".'

He's just finished another one-act play for the amateur company, and is in the early stages of developing a six-part drama for TV. He's also taking another course, this time a postgraduate qualification in Careers Guidance.

Points to consider

- Going out and making contact with people who use writing and need writers can help you promote your work.
- It can be helpful to find work outside writing that allows you flexibility.
- If you do keep writing, treating it as a job can increase your effectiveness and confidence.

Case study 6

JH left school without taking A Levels. When her daughter reached the age of 14, she signed up for three A levels (including combined English Language and Literature) at a further education college. She didn't consider applying to university until someone she knew at the college decided to do so.

Since childhood, JH had wanted to be a writer, making up stories to fit the pictures in picture-books. She applied for Creative Writing joint with English. She felt it was important to keep the literary perspective alongside the creative, and found it stimulating and 'really useful' to study books in depth with knowledgeable tutors, as well as to be introduced to works she wouldn't normally have chosen to read.

In Creative Writing, 'I didn't know what to expect, but I'd written stories for A Level and I felt very open to whatever I was asked to do. I just wanted to go on writing stories.' Her tutors were 'all great', except one who was inexperienced and dealing with a difficult group. 'Group dynamics are important; it makes a big difference if students are helping each other out, not just relying on the tutor or trying to avoid doing any work.'

She graduated in 2001, and immediately applied for and gained a place on the Creative Writing MA at the same institution, something she'd known she wanted to do from an early stage of the undergraduate course. The MA was 'fabulous'.

The novel she wrote on the MA was taken up by a London agency and offered to several publishers. 'I feel ambivalent about that, because although it's nice to be taken up, I wasn't entirely happy with the novel I'd written. In hindsight, I wonder whether I was writing more to please others than to please myself at that time.'

JH is currently doing a creative writing PhD: 'not so much for the academic qualification . . . it legitimises me sitting at home, tapping away on the computer. You have to justify the activity in a way that people can understand, so they don't think you're being useless.' There's also a 'community' aspect: 'I want to be around people who are interested in writing and interesting *about* writing.'

JH is also teaching on the undergraduate course now: 'this makes me interrogate things that I'm going to raise in class – I know students are going to ask me questions and I don't want to fall flat on my face or mislead them. It doesn't mean I have to come up with the answers, but

I have to be able to discuss things intelligently with them . . . it makes me think deeply about the subject and about my own writing process.' Teaching creative writing can be rewarding: 'It gives a great sense of achievement, using my skills to help someone else improve their writing, or if you encourage someone who's lukewarm to be enthusiastic and have confidence.'

There's also a practical aspect to JH's decision to teach: 'If you want to go on writing you've got to find a way to fund it – I don't want to spend my life in a garret with a leaking ceiling and nothing to eat . . . so teaching is valuable in bringing in money while also leaving me time to write. Teaching feeds my own writing . . . You learn things from the students too . . .'

Points to consider

- Even after you've done a course you may find it hard to call yourself a writer.
- Getting an agent does not mean you will necessarily sell your book.
- There is now a growing 'community' of writing teachers and students. This may be an area where you can both use and develop what you've learned from your course.

Case study 7

Loo Murray did creative writing 'by accident' – the General Creative Writing Workshop module was one of the options for education students, and after reading the course description she decided to 'give it a whizz'. She was unlucky enough to experience my first-ever undergraduate creative writing workshop in 1994. She writes:

> When I arrived at university I had no idea what was in store. I will never forget (my feet are tying themselves in knots at the thought) that first seminar group when you announced with a flick of your wrist that we should write about a lop-sided, black bag plonked in the middle of the room. I hadn't written anything since I was about eight. I wanted to climb into the bag, pull the drawstrings around my very tight and dry throat and kill myself, there and then – providing yet another interesting subject for the enthusiastic team of writers to elaborate on.

Loo did survive, and in fact enjoyed creative writing so much that she switched to a combined English and Creative Writing degree, graduating in 1998. She went on to start a postgraduate teaching diploma, but decided it wasn't for her (though she did get into print in the *Times Educational Supplement* with an article based on her experiences). Instead she took a Teaching Adults Certificate, and went into adult education, conducting creative writing sessions with the elderly and people with disabilities. At first she worked in several different colleges on a part-time basis, which made for a disjointed working pattern. She now works with a community learning team, delivering Family Learning programmes. This involves getting parents as well as children to write. 'I love what I do so much; part of my focus is getting people to think beyond the classroom, to get them to understand that literacy is more than just books.'

Loo now has her own magic bag, along with some old bits of fruit, sherbert lemons and corkscrews, but assures me she doesn't terrify her students in the same way that I did.

Points to consider

- As a writer you should be aware of opportunities to use your talents at all times.
- Writing, and teaching writing, can offer you career opportunities outside of publishing your work.

Case study 8

Daren King graduated in 1998. He did a combined degree in Creative Writing and English. He didn't enjoy the English much: 'I'm not really into literature. If I could play the guitar I would have joined a band instead.' He published his first novel, *Boxy an Star*, in 1999. He has since published two more novels and has worked as a journalist. Was doing the course any use to him? 'It was a long time ago so it is hard to remember. The course changed my life, as it was through the course that I found my first publisher. I am not sure I found the course that useful. I don't remember being taught the mechanics of writing, for example how to structure a sentence or a paragraph. I don't remember being taught, for example, that the last word in a sentence has the most emphasis. I learnt that sort of stuff myself from books on creative writing.'

How about tutors and fellow students? 'I'm not sure I want to get personal about people. All of the fellow students were different. Some I liked and some I didn't like. It was a very up and down sort of time. Some of it was amazing and some of it was dreadful.'

He got into journalism as a direct result of his first novel: 'One of the editors at the *Guardian* was a big fan of *Boxy an Star*. He wrote to me and suggested we meet. My first six pieces were TV reviews, the most read piece in the *Guardian*; odd when you consider that that I had no interest in TV.'

If he had his time again would he do creative writing at university? 'I found my first publisher through one of my tutors, so I would be daft to do something else. I'd be stuck in a regular job right now, or dead, or both.'

Points to consider

- Your course can be useful in a variety of ways, beyond teaching you how to write.
- You may not need a course to be able to write your first book, but the things you learn can help with your second.
- You don't have to like television to write television reviews.

Further reading

I have arranged this section to correspond to each chapter of the main text. This means that the same books may appear in several places. Wherever possible, I have tried to limit references to those works that I feel will be of direct interest to a student of creative writing, though there are occasional pointers towards sources dealing with statistics and pedagogical issues. As with any other discipline, my suggestion would be that you read as much as you possibly can, and read it with an open but critical mind, always with the aim of improving your writing and clarifying your thinking about your own writing, and writing in general.

1 Creative writing: can it be taught?

Can you teach writing?

Margaret Atwood's *Negotiating with the Dead* (London, Virago, 2003) deals thoughtfully and interestingly with the subject of writing and being a writer. She also touches on the parallels between training as a musician and (not) training as a writer.

Alan Ayckbourn begins his highly entertaining and useful *The Crafty Art of Playmaking* (London, Faber, 2002) with the disclaimer that writing 'can never in any strict sense be "taught" '; however, the rest of the book proves that there's an awful lot an experienced and reflective writer can pass on to someone learning the crafty art. His objection to the teaching of writing lies more in the fact that it's not an exact science.

Craft and mystery

For a down-to-earth and entertaining account of the romantic myth of the mysterious writer, see Heather Leach's chapter 'Creativity' in *The Road to Somewhere* (Basingstoke, Palgrave Macmillan, 2005, pp.18–27). For a full treatment of the whole question see Rob Pope's *Creativity* (Abingdon, Routledge, 2005). His discussion of 'creation vs production' (p.7f) is particularly relevant.

It's worth reading Henry James's 'The Art of Fiction' (first published in *Longman's Magazine* 4, September 1884, and reprinted in *Partial Portraits*, Macmillan, 1888) in its entirety. I found it at http:// www.thevalve.org/go/valve/article/file_under_unsurprising/ (accessed 16th August 2005) where there is also interesting discussion of the issues involved in the art of writing.

For a poetic perspective on starting to write, try Ted Hughes *Poetry in the Making* (London, Faber, 1967).

If you want to try some of the 'non-creative' writing guides mentioned in this chapter, details are as follows: *Strategies for Successful Writing: A Rhetoric, Research Guide, Reader and Handbook*, James A. Reinking, Andrew W. Hart, Robert von der Osten (Prentice Hall, 2001); *The Simon and Schuster Handbook for Writers*, Lynn Quitman Troyka (Prentice Hall, 2001).

2 Creative writing: why take a university course?

What makes a degree course different

Julia Bell, in *The Creative Writing Coursebook* (Basingstoke, Macmillan, 2001, p.xii), characterises the special qualities of an academic course as lying in the 'relationship between a critical and creative discourse'. Jane Rogers, 'Teaching the craft of writing', in Moira Monteith and Robert Miles (eds) *Teaching Creative Writing* (Buckingham, Open University Press, 1992, pp.108–119) stresses that the 'craft' element of writing is essential in an academic context. Paul Dawson gives an in-depth account of the characteristics of creative writing in universities in *Creative Writing and the New Humanities* (Abingdon, Routledge, 2005).

Validation or accreditation

In the US, although individual institutions have relative autonomy, most reputable courses will have some kind of external accreditation. You can find out all about this subject on the US government Department of Education website: http://www.ed.gov/admins/finaid/accred/index.html (accessed 7 December 2006). The Council on Higher Education Accreditation (www.chea.org) operates to recognise private, non-governmental courses. Also relevant (and at times inspirational) are the Association of Writers and Writing Programs Hallmarks of a Successful Undergraduate Program in Creative Writing: http://www.awpwriter.org (accessed 10 December 2006):

> For undergraduate writers, a good four-year curriculum requires more general studies of literature, the arts and sciences, and the fine arts; it also provides extracurricular experiences in writing, publishing, and literature . . . Because a writer must first become a voracious and expert reader before he or she can master a difficult art, a strong undergraduate program emphasizes a wide range of study in literature and other disciplines to provide students with the foundation they need to become resourceful writers – resourceful in techniques, styles, models, ideas, and subject matter. The goal of an undergraduate program is to teach students how to read critically as writers and to give students the practice of writing frequently so that, by creating their own works, they may apply what they have learned about the elements of literature.

In Australia the monitoring of course standards comes under the *Higher Education Quality Assurance Framework*, details of which can be found at http://www.aqf.edu.au/quality.htm (accessed 7 December 2006).

Miscellaneous

On the importance of mess, see John Singleton, 'The necessity of mess', in *The Road to Somewhere* (Basingstoke, Palgrave Macmillan, 2005, pp.28–35), and for 'postponing perfection', see Linda Anderson *Creative Writing: A Workbook with Readings* (Abingdon, Routledge, 2006, for the Open University, p.21f).

For a good introduction to the 'Death of the author', see Robert Eaglestone, *Doing English* (London, Routledge, 2000, pp.76f and 151). Barthes' essay first appeared in *Image, Music, Text* (ed. and trans. Stephen Heath (New York, Hill and Wang, 1971). You can find it in Sean Burke's *Authorship from Plato to the Postmodern* (Edinburgh, Edinburgh University Press, 1995).

3 Creative writing now

Some of the material of this chapter will appear in a slightly different form in 'Undergraduate creative writing provision in the UK: origins, trends and student views', in *Teaching Creative Writing in Higher Education: Anglo-American Perspectives*, edited by Heather Beck (to be published by Palgrave as part of the Teaching the New English series).

Finding out about courses

In the UK a good place to start if you want to find out about university-based courses is the Universities and Colleges Admissions Service (UCAS) website course search facility, to be found at http://www.ucas.com/search/index.html (accessed 13 November 2005). Try searching for 'Writing', then 'Creative Writing', 'Imaginative Writing', 'Fiction', 'Poetry', 'Scriptwriting', and, for good measure, 'Professional Writing'.

The Arts Council of Great Britain operates a site dealing with all kinds of educational opportunities in the field of writing: http://literature.hciyork.co.uk (accessed 13 November 2005).

In the USA you can find courses via the Association of Writers and Writing Programs (AWP): http://www.awpwriter.org/ (accessed 24 October 2006). The AWP *Official Guide to Writing Programs*, 'contains information on 300 graduate programs, 400 undergraduate programs, and 250 writers' conferences, festivals, and centers'. In the introduction to this useful publication, David Fenza points out the variety of kinds of course in the US:

In some programs, students must satisfy many traditional requirements for literary scholarship: proficiency in one or more foreign languages; distribution requirements in the arts, sciences, and humanities; an overview of literature from three or more centuries; and a command of scholarly research and documentation skills. Other programs have few of these requirements, if any, as the emphasis is mainly on the progress of the student's writing.

In Australia, university admissions are handled on a state by state basis. So, for example, for courses in New South Wales try the Universities Admissions Centre site: http://www.uac.edu.au/. My own search for creative writing courses there (accessed 25 October 2006) yielded 80 results, throwing up a huge variety of degree programmes including International Studies, Performance, Cultural Studies, Public Relations, Psychology, Sports Media, Journalism, Advertising, Marketing and Commerce. It's therefore unsurprising that the site's front page bears the plaintive message, 'many applicants have applied for the wrong types of courses'.

The growth of creative writing

For an interesting account of the history of creative writing in the US and UK, and the variety of courses on offer, see Lauri Ramey, 'Creative writing and English studies: two approaches to literature', available at http://www.english.heacademy.ac.uk/archive/events/cwriting/Ramey.rtf (accessed 12 December 2006).

UK statistics are taken from the English Subject Centre *Survey of the English Curriculum and Teaching in UK Higher Education* (Halcrow Group Limited, 2003) with Jane Gawthrope and Professor Philip Martin, available at http://www.english.heacademy.ac.uk/archive/publications/reports/curr_teach_main.pdf (accessed 16 August 2005), and also the Higher Education Statistics Agency statistics (http://www.hesa.ac.uk/). There, 'Imaginative writing' first appears as a subject in its own right in 2002/3 with 775 full-time undergraduate students. This rises to 1200 in the most recent (2003/4) figures (accessed 25 January 2006).

For US statistics, see http://nces.ed.gov, and Marjorie Perloff, ' "Creative Writing" among the Disciplines,' *MLA Newsletter* 38(1) (2006): 3–4, which also addresses many of the questions of the nature of creative writing as an academic discipline.

For Australia, see Paul Dawson *Creative Writing and the New Humanities* (Abingdon, Routledge, 2005, Chapter 4, p.121f).

Writers and teachers

The National Association of Writers in Education (NAWE) has an area on its website www.nawe.co.uk (accessed 13 November 2005), dedicated to Writing at University, with some useful articles and case studies. If you are really interested in the debates about the role of writers in the academy, then you could join NAWE and access their archives, where pieces by Vicki Feaver, Terry Gifford, Philip Gross and Jeremy Hooker address the issue. For one academic's journey to enlightenment, see Nick Everett, 'Creative writing and English', *Cambridge Quarterly*, 35 (4), 231–42.

You could also try my own analysis of 'Undergraduate creative writing provision in the UK: origins, trends and student views', in *Teaching Creative Writing in Higher Education: Anglo-American Perspectives*, edited by Heather Beck (Palgrave, forthcoming), part of the Teaching the New English series).

For a US perspective, see David Myers, *The Elephants Teach: Creative Writing Since 1880* (Chicago University Press, 1996, new edition 2006). Lauri Ramey, 'Creative writing and English studies: two approaches to literature', available at http://www.english.heacademy.ac.uk/archive/events/cwriting/Ramey.rtf (accessed 12 December 2006), deals with the tensions between 'literature' academics and creative writing tutors entertainingly:

> A common perception among those involved in literature is that Creative Writers and Creative Writing programmes are flighty. Insubstantial. Non-pragmatic. Navel-gazing. Engaged in useless play that should have been set aside in childhood . . . a haven for impractical starry-eyed infantile dreamers.

This article is also the source of the 'unreliable troublemakers' quotation.

For Australia, see Paul Dawson *Creative Writing and the New Humanities* (Abingdon, Routledge, 2005, pp.123–4).

4 How courses are organised and how you will learn

Starter course books

Linda Anderson's *Creative Writing: A Workbook with Readings* (Abingdon, Routledge, 2006) is designed for students starting creative writing with the Open University in the UK. These courses, recently introduced, have proved immensely popular, but at the time of writing are only available at Level 2.

The *Creative Writer's Handbook*, edited by Philip K. Jason and Allan B. Lefcowitz (Prentice-Hall, 2004) and Candace H. Schaefer and Rick Diamond *The Creative Writing Guide: A Path to Poetry, Nonfiction and Drama* (Longman, 1998), are designed more with US creative writing introductory courses in mind.

The Creative Writing Coursebook, edited by Julia Bell and Paul Magrs (Basingstoke, Macmillan, 2001), is based on the collected wisdom of teachers at both undergraduate and postgraduate level based at the University of East Anglia in the UK.

Paul Mills' *The Routledge Creative Writing Coursebook* (Abingdon, Routledge, 2006) and Janet Burraway's *Imaginative Writing: The Elements of Craft* (Longman, 2002) also give general coverage of the main genres of writing useful for anyone taking a general introduction to creative writing.

Workshops

Stephanie Vanderslice, 'Workshopping', in *Teaching Creative Writing*, edited by Graeme Harper (London, Continuum, 2006, p.147f), discusses the benefits, drawbacks and purposes of workshops.

Two chapters in Moira Monteith and Robert Miles (eds), *Teaching Creative Writing* (Buckingham, Open University Press, 1992) deal with workshops: Philip Hobsbaum, 'The teaching of creative writing' (pp.24–33), and Michael Mangan, 'Methodizing: drama and creative writing', (pp.131–43), which discusses workshop games and exercises. On the other hand, Robert Sheppard, 'The poetics of writing: the writing of poetics', NAWE archive, argues against student 'dependence on workshop activity' for stimulus, and in a much earlier article, Don Bogen, 'Beyond the workshop: suggestions for a process-orientated creative writing course', *JAC 5.0* (1988), available at http://jac.gsu.edu/jac/5.1/Articles/13.htm (accessed 20 November 2005), advances the argument, echoed in some press articles recently, that workshops tend 'by nature to encourage the slick but shallow work we deplore ... this type of class produces not only "workshop" pieces but "workshop" *writers*. It gives students a false idea of what writers do and why they do it.'

The Creative Writing Coursebook, edited by Julia Bell and Paul Magrs (Basingstoke, Macmillan, 2001) has a section devoted to workshops (pp.292–319).

Siobhan Holland's *Creative Writing: A Good Practice Guide: A Report to the Learning and Teaching Support Network (LTSN)* (English Subject Centre, 2003) can be found on line at: http://www.english.ltsn.ac.uk/explore/resources/creative/guide.php (accessed 20 November 2005). Page 6 stresses the importance of 'support services' for students 'who may well draw on traumatic experiences in the processes of reading and writing'. For another, succinct, US perspective see Janet Burroway and Elizabeth Stuckey-French, *Writing Fiction: A Guide to Narrative Craft* (Longman, 2006, pp. xi-xiv).

Statistics

UK statistics come from the Higher Education Statistics Agency, which can be found at http://www.hesa.ac.uk (accessed 31 December 2005). Because of the difficulty of finding and defining creative writing courses and elements in courses at the moment no figures can pretend to be accurate.

In the US, the National Center for Educational Statistics has some interesting material, to be found at nces.ed.gov (accessed 7 December 2006), as does the Australian Department of Education, Science and Training website: http://www.dest.gov.au (accessed 7 December 2006).

5 Assessment

You can find a couple of specimen 'non-creative' assessment pieces in *The Road to Somewhere* (Basingstoke, Palgrave Macmillan, 2005, pp.282–90).

Russell Celyn Jones gives a tutor's perspective on assessment in *The Creative Writing Coursebook*, edited by Julia Bell and Paul Magrs (Basingstoke, Macmillan, 2001, pp.245–8).

George Marsh explores some of the issues in '43%: A commentary on aims and assessment in the teaching of literary writing', in *Teaching Creative Writing* (Buckingham, Open University Press, 1992), edited by Moira Monteith and Robert Miles, pp.45–58. If you want a more formal perspective, you could try Ann Atkinson, Liz Cashdan, Livi Michael and Ian Pople, 'Analysing the aesthetic: a new approach to developing criteria for the assessment of creative writing in higher education', *Writing in Education*, 21 (Winter 2000/01), pp.26–8, or Keith Green 'Creative writing, language and evaluation', Working Papers on the Web, Vol. 2 (Sheffield Hallam University, 2001) http://www.shu.ac.uk/wpw/value/green.htm (accessed 9 December 2005).

For the growing perceived importance of assessment criteria in the US, see the NCES (National Postsecondary Education Cooperative) Student Outcomes Pilot Working Group *Sourcebook on Assessment, Volume 1*, available at http://nces.ed.gov/pubs2000/2000195.pdf (accessed 13 December 2006). In excess of 100 criteria are listed for 'dimensions of writing', including 'Awareness and knowledge of audience', and the ability to 'draw on [students'] own individual creativity to engage their audience' (p.46). In Australia, too, 'the reliance on tacit values – tacit notions of quality – is giving way to calls for transparency of process, for public access to the bases of judgment, for the articulation of criteria' (*The Australian*, 13 November 1996, p.58).

6 Developing your own writing habits

Writers' habits

I've taken examples of writers' working methods from several sources, including *How Novelists Work*, edited by Maura Dooley (Bridgend, Seren Books, 2000) and *The Author* (the Journal of the Society of Authors), which carries an occasional series of articles by authors about their working methods. James Carter's *Talking Books: Children's Authors Talk About the Craft, Creativity and Process of Writing* (Routledge, 1999) is also very informative.

Creative Writing: A Workbook with Readings, edited by Linda Anderson (Abingdon, Routledge, 2006 for the Open University) has an extensive and interesting section of 'Readings', consisting of short extracts by writers dealing with all aspects of the creative and writing process. It also contains a useful chapter on the practicalities of keeping a writer's notebook (pp.33–43).

Research

For an entertaining view of research see Graeme Harper's 'Research in creative writing' in *Teaching Creative Writing*, edited by Graeme Harper (London, Continuum, 2006, p.158f).

Story, by Robert McKee (London, Methuen, 1999), though principally aimed at screenwriters, has excellent material about how a writer should approach their material. See, for example, the sections on research (p.72f) and creative choices (aka editing, p.76f).

7 Writing and editing

Revision and editing

Creative Writing: A Workbook with Readings, edited by Linda Anderson (Abingdon, Routledge, 2006 for the Open University), has two chapters by Sara Haslam on different levels of editing (pp.359–82), covering 'big changes' and 'later stages'.

In Paul Mills' *The Routledge Creative Writing Coursebook* (Abingdon, Routledge, 2006), each section is devoted to a different kind of writing and concludes with suggestions for appropriate 'Revision and Editing'.

There is a short, but useful, editing checklist in Ailsa Cox, *Writing Short Stories* (Abingdon, Routledge, 2005, p.169f), in the section on erotic fiction.

There's a useful section on Revising in *The Creative Writing Coursebook*, edited by Julia Bell and Paul Magrs (Basingstoke, Macmillan, 2001), with pieces by Paul Magrs, Lindsay Clarke, James Friel, Vicki Feaver and Julia Bell (pp.251–91); or you could look at my own 'Scriptwriting for radio', in *Teaching Creative Writing*, edited by Graeme Harper (London, Continuum, 2006, p.91f).

See also Janet Burroway and Elizabeth Stuckey-French, *Writing Fiction: A Guide to Narrative Craft* (Longman, 2006, p.388f) and Janet Burroway, *Imaginative Writing: The Elements of Craft* (Longman, 2006).

Our reluctant student editors may well have been influenced by David Cronenberg's 1991 film *Naked Lunch* (based, loosely, on the William Burroughs novel), in which characters debate whether 'rewriting is really censorship':

> See, you can't rewrite, 'cause to rewrite is to deceive and lie, and you betray your own thoughts. To rethink the flow and the rhythm, the tumbling out of the words, is a betrayal, and it's a sin.

Presentation

For the importance of, and advice about, presentation see Mary Hammond's chapter 'Presentation and proposal' in *Creative Writing: a Workbook with Readings*, edited by Linda Anderson (Abingdon, Routledge, 2006 for the Open University, pp.397–410).

Miscellaneous

If you haven't read it, I'd recommend Hunter S. Thompson, *Fear and Loathing in Las Vegas* (Harper Perennial Modern Classics, 2005), as a breath of fresh air in terms of narrative voice. It's also worth noting that he apparently took two years turning the raw idea into something coherent.

The editor of 'Too Much for Normous', published as *The Fish Fly Low* (London, Methuen, 1993, reissued 1997 as *Friendly Fire*) was the wonderful Miriam Hodgson, who died while I was writing this book. If you've read books by Anne Fine, Helen Dunmore, Geraldine McCaughrean, Robert Westall, Jenny Nimmo, or a host of other popular writers for young people, the chances are that Miriam edited many of them. You can also sample her editing prowess in a series of short story collections, such as *Heart to Heart* (London, Mammoth, 1996) and *Love from Dad* (London, Egmont, 2002).

Conclusion: beyond the course

Further study

One good resource for anyone considering an MFA in the US is Tom Kealey, *The Creative Writing MFA Handbook* (London, Continuum, 2005). See also Amy Holman, *An Insider's Guide to Creative Writing Programs: Choosing the Right MFA or MA Program, Colony, Residency, Grant or Fellowship* (Prentice-Hall, 2006).

Reference books

The two 'bibles' in the UK for writers looking for outlets for their work are *The Writers' and Artists' Yearbook* (London, A & C Black) and *The Writers' Handbook* (London, Macmillan). These are revised annually, so try to get the most up-to-date version. They give lists of agents, publishers, broadcasters, reference prizes and resources, and also give practical tips.

In the US, *Writer's Market* (Writer's Digest Books, annual), edited by Robert Lee Brewer, and *The Writer's Handbook* (Writer Inc. annual), edited by Elfreida Abbe, fulfil a similar function.

Advice about getting published, or what to do if you can't

There's a useful section on the mechanics of trying to get published in *The Creative Writing Coursebook*, edited by Julia Bell and Paul Magrs (Basingstoke, Macmillan, 2001), with pieces by Julia Bell, Julian Jackson, Rebecca Swift, Candi Miller, Penny Rendall and Paul Magrs (pp.320–74).

There are two good chapters on 'Getting published' (John Singleton) and 'How not being published can change your life' (Heather Leach) in *The Road to Somewhere* (Basingstoke, Palgrave Macmillan, 2005, pp.245–54 and pp.262–71). In the latter, the writer suggests lots of ways you can use your writing (and improve it) outside of commercial publishing.

See also Mary Hammond's chapter 'Exploring outlets' in *Creative Writing: A Workbook with Readings*, edited by Linda Anderson (Abingdon, Routledge, 2006, for the Open University, pp.383–96).

For a US-orientated view, try *The Complete Handbook of Novel Writing: Everything You Need to Know About Creating and Selling Your Work*, by

Meg Leder and Jack Heffron (Writer's Digest Books, 2002). The Writer's Digest site is also full of helpful links: http://www.writersdigest.com (accessed 7 December 2006).

Courses and writers' groups

The most famous provider of short writing courses in the UK is the Arvon Foundation, 42a Buckingham Palace Road, London SW1W 0RE, which runs four centres offering five-day courses covering a variety of writing genres and topics (http://www.arvonfoundation.org). Funding support is also available.

On-line classes are available, for example at http://www.writers.com.

Many universities run short writing classes as part of their Continuing Education or Lifelong Learning programmes. You can look for information about these in your local university prospectus or (in the UK) try http://www.niace.org.uk (the National Institute of Adult Continuing Education).

You may find writers' groups in your local library or in evening class programmes. You can look for a local group at http://www.nawg.co.uk (the National Association of Writers' Groups). I found useful lists of groups at http://www.oneofus.co.uk/writers_directory/uk_writing_groups.htm and http://www.writerswrite.com/groups.htm. (accessed 28 December 2005).

You could try an online group such as The Short Story Group (http://www.shortstorygroup.com).

The BBC Writersroom (www.bbc.co.uk/writersroom) has lots of information about how to get started in writing for broadcast media (it's not easy).

Scriptwriter magazine is full of useful articles and contacts (available on-line at http://www.scriptwritermagazine.com (accessed 5 February 2006).

http://www.writersservices.com/mag/.htm (accessed 18 January 2006) offers a listing of useful organisations, and you can subscribe for free to the entertaining Writers' Services e-newsletter.

Index